PRACTISE & PASS 11+

MATHS
PRACTICE PAPERS

Contents

⚙ Practice paper 1	3
⚙ Practice paper 2	17
⚙ Practice paper 3	33
⚙ Practice paper 4	49

© Peter Williams and Trotman Publishing, 2015

The right of Peter Williams to be identified as the author of this work has been asserted by him in accordance with the Copyright, Designs and Patents Act, 1988.

All rights reserved. No part of this publication may be transmitted in any form or by any means, or stored in a retrieval system without prior written permission from the publisher.

First published 2015 by Trotman Publishing, a division of Crimson Publishing Ltd, 19–21c Charles Street, Bath BA1 1HX.

ISBN 978 1 84455 428 7

A catalogue record for this book is available from the British Library.

PRACTISE AND PASS 11+

MATHS
MULTIPLE CHOICE

PRACTICE PAPER 1

Read the following instructions carefully.

1. Do <u>not</u> begin until you are told to do so.
2. This is a multiple choice test.
3. Answers should be marked on the answer grids provided.
4. Mark your answer in the corresponding answer grid by drawing a firm line clearly in the rectangle next to your answer.
5. If you make a mistake, make sure you rub it out completely before marking a new answer. There should be only one answer marked for each question.
6. You may do any working out on a separate sheet of paper.
7. Make sure you keep your place on the answer grids.
8. Work quickly and carefully. If you cannot do a question, move on to the next one and come back to it later.
9. A calculator may <u>not</u> be used.
10. You will have 50 minutes to complete this test.

1 Which value does the 3 in 120,301 represent?

---

2 Classes in Year 6 sell vouchers for charity. The results are shown in the table below.

Key: 🎟 = 5 vouchers   🎟 = fewer than 5 vouchers

Class	Vouchers collected
6A	🎟 🎟 🎟 🎟 🎟
6B	🎟 🎟 🎟 🎟 🎟(small)
6C	🎟 🎟 🎟
6D	🎟 🎟(small)
6E	🎟 🎟 🎟 🎟(small)

What is the difference between the number of vouchers Class 6A sold and the number of vouchers Class 6E sold?

---

3 Of 720 books in a local book shop, $\frac{2}{9}$ are non-fiction and the rest are fiction. How many books are fiction?

---

4 The table below shows the percentage of vehicles that were recorded travelling past a school during one week.

Type of Vehicle	Car	Van	Bike	Truck	Bus
Percentage	33%	14%	17%	9%	?

What percentage of the vehicles observed were buses?

5 Mr Khan sells bunches of daffodils in the local market. On Thursday he sold 25 bunches and made £19.50. For how much did he sell each bunch?

6 A garden path is 3m long. Mr Walsh decides to put 9 lights at equal spaces apart along his path. How many centimetres apart does each light need to be?

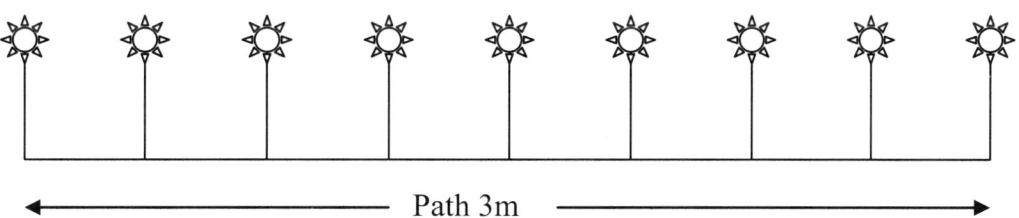

Path 3m

7 The table below shows the number of people who visited the seaside town of Tranquilling during the summer months each year.

Year	2005	2006	2007	2008	2009	2010
Number of people visiting	120	219	276	174	209	271

What was the range of the number of visitors across the 6 years?

8 A supermarket has 23 aisles of items for sale and 79 items are bought from each aisle each hour. How many items are bought in total each hour?

9 Which of the following shapes has a vertical line of symmetry?

A  B   C  D 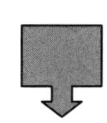 E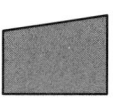

Go straight on to the next page

10 The grid below shows a local parkland area.

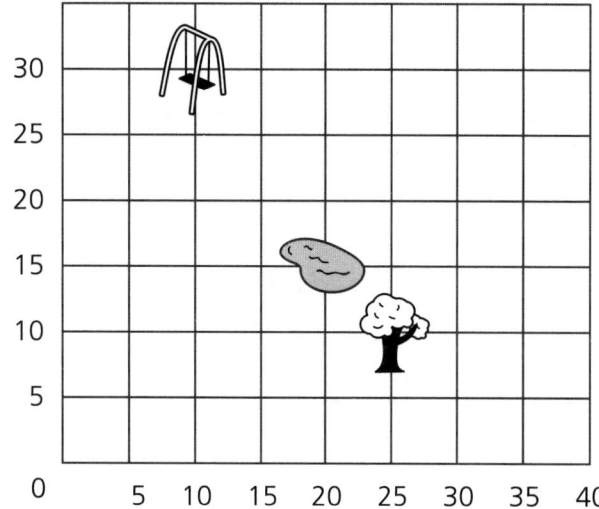

Where is the pond located?

---

11 The children in Scribo Primary School are making a magazine. If they have 30 pictures for the magazine and these represent $\frac{2}{5}$ of the total pages, how many pages does the magazine have altogether?

---

12 The perimeter of a rectangle is 24cm. If two of its sides each measure 9cm, what is the area of the rectangle?

---

13 This machine subtracts 7 then multiplies by 9.

19 → 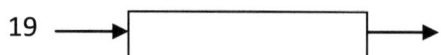 →

Which number comes out?

Go straight on to the next page

14 Look at the grid below. Each of the letters X, Y and Z represents a number. Each row, column and diagonal adds up to 9.

Josh knows that the letter X is worth more than the letter Z.
What is the value of letter Z?

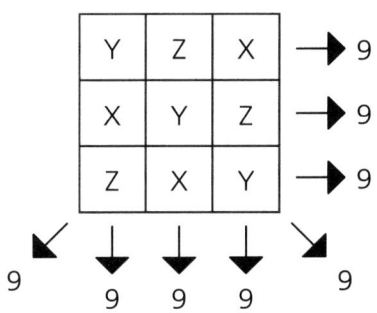

15 Tommy has a cactus plant. He decides to measure it using his school ruler. The cactus measures 23.349cm. He decides to round this to two decimal places. What is his new measurement?

16 Four A4-sized folders placed together end to end are the same length as a table. Which length is the table most likely to be?

A 2 metres
B 0.3 metres
C 300 centimetres
D 30 centimetres
E 1.2 metres

17 3 years ago Elizabeth's cousin was x years old. How old will she be in 5 years' time?

18 Dilip is a keen wildlife enthusiast. He notes the number of birds which visit his garden. In one week he noted that 98 birds visited his garden and $\frac{4}{7}$ of these were bluebirds. How many bluebirds visited his garden in that week?

19 Leila and Carmel raised money for charity by helping out their neighbours. They managed to raise £118 between them but Carmel raised £14 more than Leila. How much money did Carmel raise?

Go straight on to the next page

20 The children at Goodwill Primary School bake cakes to be sold for charity. If each cakes costs 13p to make and they sell them for 20p, how much profit do they make if they sell 87 cakes?

21 The local health centre is holding its annual cross-country race. Everyone has to run around the outside of the fields shown below and Joseph has to let everyone know how far they have to run. How far has everyone run when they have completed 1 lap?

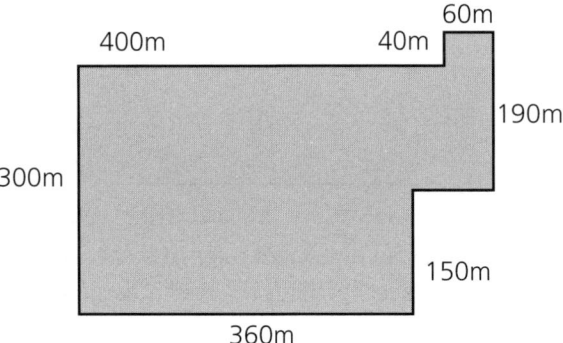

22 Which of the shapes below does not have rotational symmetry?

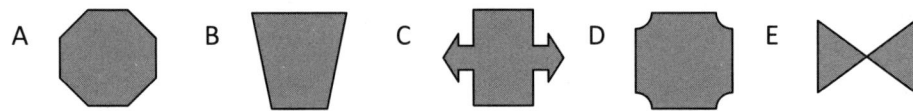

23 Which number is a multiple of both 7 and 4?

24 A number is multiplied by 7. The answer is halved then trebled. The result is 63. What was the initial number?

Go straight on to the next page

25 The table below shows the prices of food at a café.

Item	Cost
Cheese roll	75p
Sausage roll	85p
Ham roll	80p
Salad roll	75p
Extra pickle	10p
Extra mustard	15p

Mr Gale buys a cheese roll with extra pickle, his wife has a salad roll and his 3 children each have a cheese roll. How much does their order come to in total?

26 April ate 3 segments of the chocolate bar below. What percentage remained?

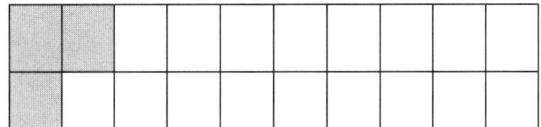

27 Gabrielle's aunt bought her a new scarf. The scarf originally cost £18.50 but was reduced by 30%. How much did Gabrielle's aunt actually pay for it?

28 The graph below shows the number of children in a school who were learning to swim each week during the term.

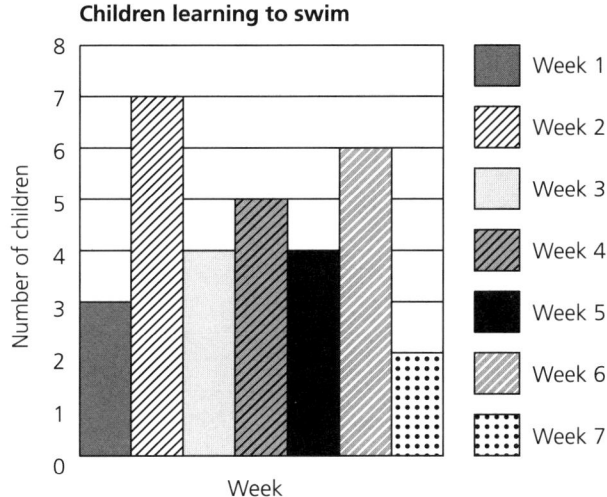

What is the mode?

29 Fran needs to replace the batteries in her son's toy car. It requires 4 batteries placed end to end and each is 25mm in length. Additionally, there is a space of 7mm between batteries and also at each end of the battery compartment. How long is the battery compartment?

30

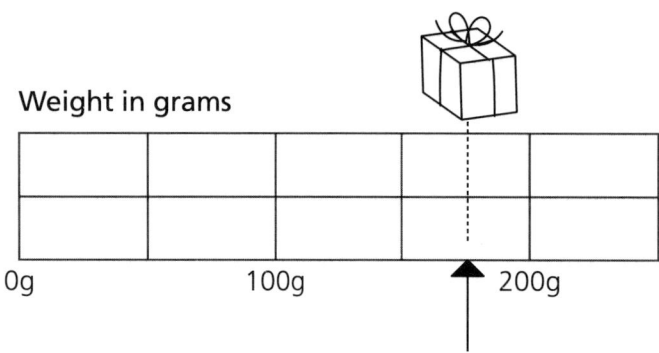

How much does the parcel weigh?

31

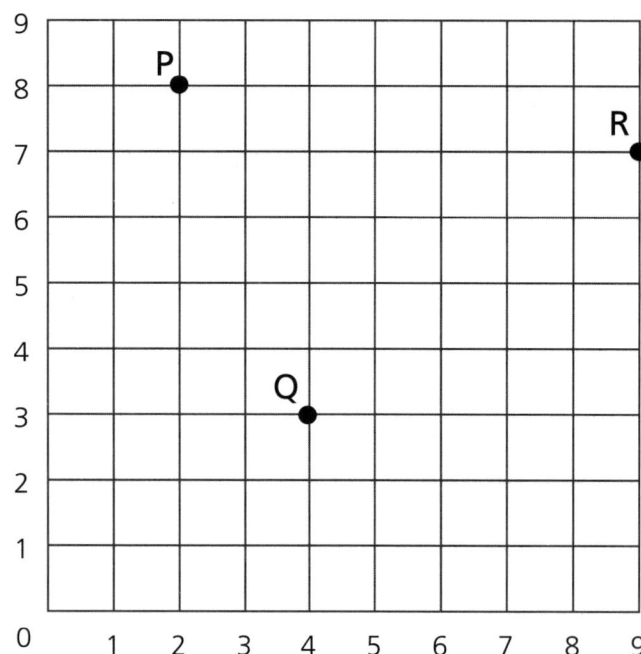

Which are the correct coordinates for points P, Q and R?

32 Trey has decided to get a new mobile phone. He will be charged s pounds to buy the phone and t pounds each month as part of his contract. How much money will he have to pay for 1 year?

Go straight on to the next page

33 Kerri is part way through reading a book with 380 pages. She has read 85% of the book. How many pages remain for her to read?

34

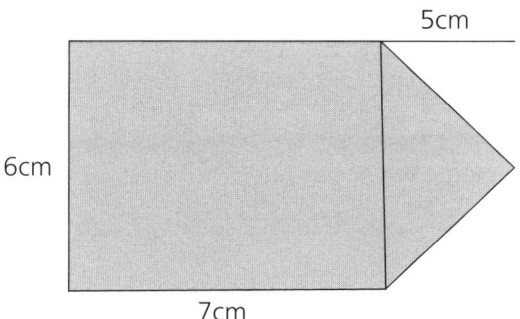

What is the area of the shape above?

35 2a + 3b − 3c = x

If a = 6, b = 7 and c = 8, what is x?

36 What is the difference between 4^2 and 4^3?

37 Which one of these gives the answer 40?

A   10% of 4000
B $\frac{3}{5}$ of 60
C $\frac{4}{9}$ of 90
D   75% of 80
E $\frac{3}{4}$ of 70

38 To win a prize at the hook-a-duck stall at the fair, children catch ducks at random with their fishing hooks. The ducks give different prizes. 5 ducks give a teddy prize, 3 give a water gun and 2 give a pack of cards.

If you catch a duck at random, in which <u>one</u> of the following are <u>both</u> statements true?

- A You have a better than even chance of catching a duck.
  You have an even chance of winning a pack of cards.
- B You are certain to catch a duck.
  You have a better than even chance of winning a water gun.
- C You are certain to catch a duck.
  You are unlikely to win a pack of cards.
- D You are certain to catch a duck.
  You are unlikely to win a teddy.
- E You are certain to catch a duck.
  You are likely to win a water gun.

39 Which of the following triangles does <u>not</u> contain an obtuse angle?

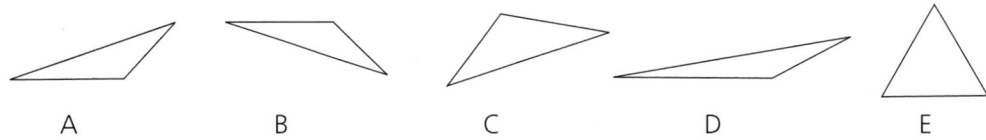

A   B   C   D   E

40 Victoria went on holiday and returned with some souvenirs. She bought a hat for $9.00 and a pen for $2.50. When she got home she calculated that the hat would have cost her £6.00 and the pen would have cost her £1.67. How much would a T shirt costing $14.00 cost her in pounds?

41 Veronica draws a quadrilateral. It has two pairs of two equal angles, one pair of parallel lines and two equal lines. What is the name of her quadrilateral?

Go straight on to the next page

42 Karen is lost in the maze. Fortunately her friend Naomi can see where she is and can tell her directions to leave the maze. Which set of directions below will get Karen from the centre C of the maze to the exit E?

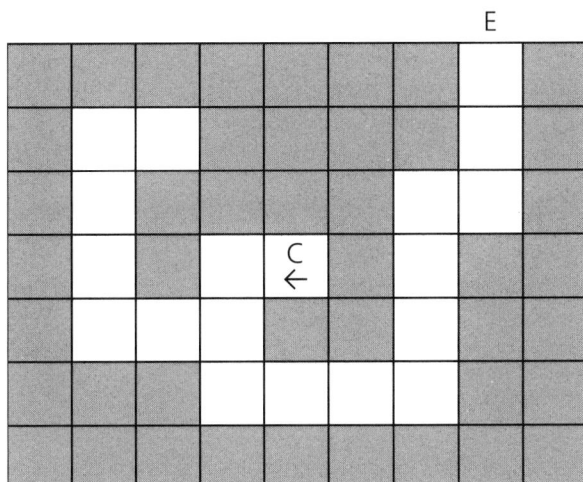

A   Forward 1, Left 90°, Forward 1, Right 90°, Forward 2, Right 90°, Forward 3, Right 90°, Forward 1.

B   Forward 1, Left 90°, Forward 2, Left 90°, Forward 3, Left 90°, Forward 3, Left 90°, Forward 1, Left 90°, Forward 2.

C   Forward 1, Left 90°, Forward 2, Left 90°, Forward 3, Left 90°, Forward 3, Right 90°, Forward 1, Left 90°, Forward 2.

D   Forward 1, Left 90°, Forward 2, Left 90°, Forward 3, Left 90°, Forward 3, Right 90°, Forward 3, Left 90°, Forward 2.

E   Forward 1, Left 90°, Forward 4, Left 90°, Forward 3, Left 90°, Forward 3, Right 90°, Forward 3, Left 90°, Forward 2.

---

43 The children in Coborn Primary School record how many books they read in a month. Their results are shown on the table below.

1–2 books	3–4 books	5–6 books	7–8 books	9–10 books	11 or more books

How many children read fewer than 7 books?

44 A map of Finland is drawn to a scale of 1:200,000. What real distance is represented by 1.5cm on the map?

45 In a local stationery shop rulers cost the same as rubbers. Rubbers cost half as much as ink pens. 4 of the following cost the same; which set does <u>not</u> cost the same as the others?

    A   3 rubbers, 2 rulers, 1 ink pen
    B   3 ink pens, 1 rubber
    C   2 ink pens, 2 rulers, 1 rubber
    D   2 ink pens, 3 rubbers
    E   1 ink pen, 3 rulers, 1 rubber

46 In the diagram below, each square represents 1cm². What is the combined area of the two shapes below?

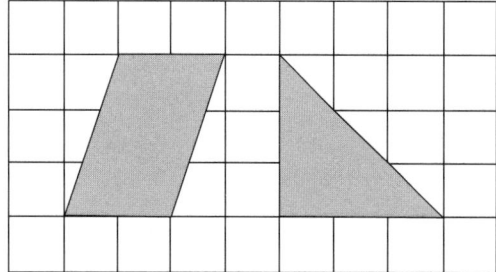

47 A right-angled triangle has 2 angles that are the same size. What size are these 2 angles?

48 Which of the following shapes has 8 edges and 5 faces?

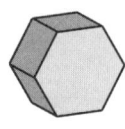 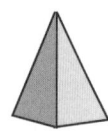 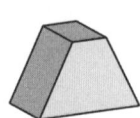  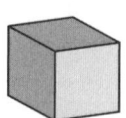

    P   Q   R   S   T

49 If (37 − 15) × 25 = 550

Which of the following is incorrect?

A 22 × 25 = 550
B 550 = (37 − 15) × 25
C 550 ÷ 25 = 37 − 15
D 550 = 22 + 15 × 25
E 25 × 22 = 550

---

50 Theo used this decision tree to sort a stack of chairs at school.

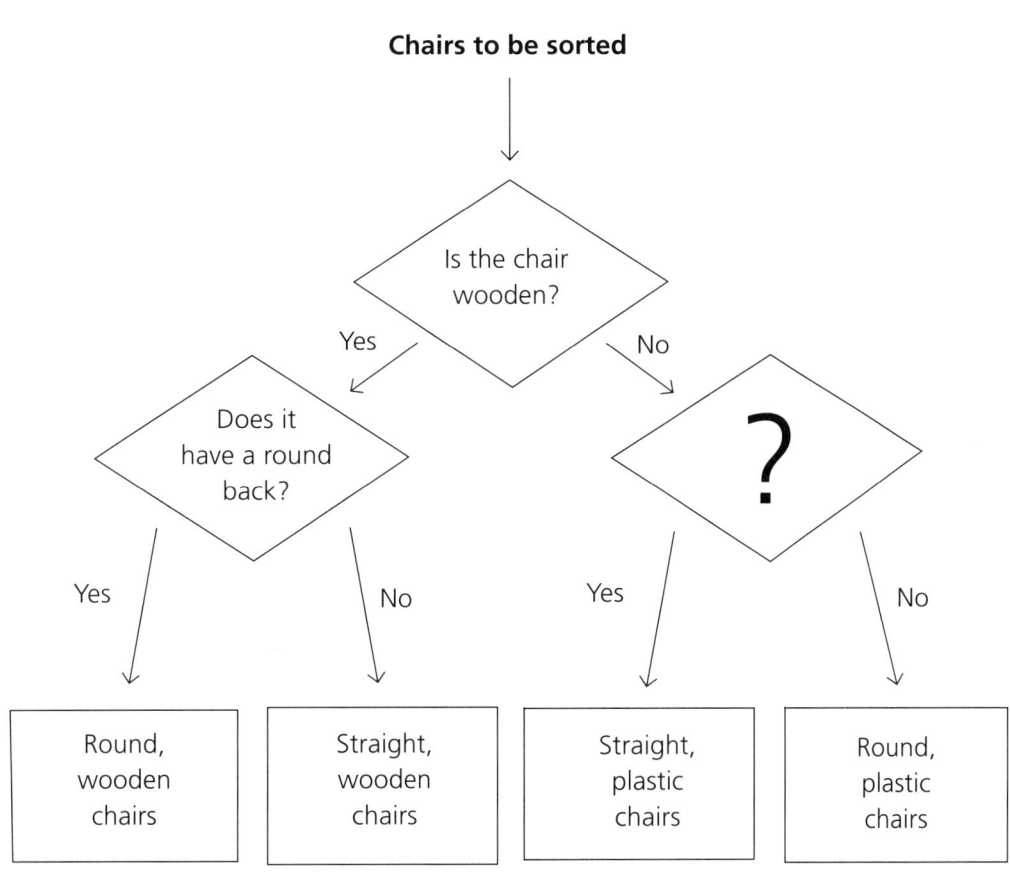

What is missing from the empty shape?

A Is it plastic?
B Does it have a round back?
C Does it have a straight back?
D Is it a chair?
E Straight, plastic chairs.

END OF TEST - PLEASE CHECK ALL YOUR ANSWERS

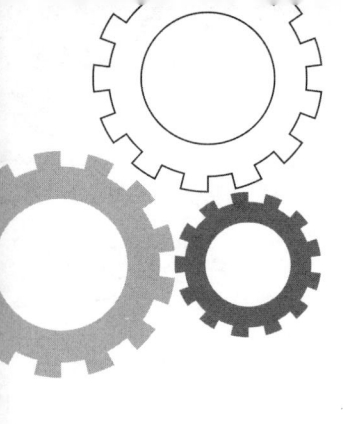

PRACTISE & PASS 11+

MATHS
MULTIPLE CHOICE

PRACTICE PAPER 2

Read the following instructions carefully.

1. Do not begin until you are told to do so.
2. This is a multiple choice test.
3. Answers should be marked on the answer grids provided.
4. Mark your answer in the corresponding answer grid by drawing a firm line clearly in the rectangle next to your answer.
5. If you make a mistake, make sure you rub it out completely before marking a new answer. There should only be one answer marked for each question.
6. You may do any working out on a separate sheet of paper.
7. Make sure you keep your place on the answer grids.
8. Work quickly and carefully. If you cannot do a question, move on to the next one and come back to it later.
9. A calculator may not be used.
10. You will have 50 minutes to complete this test.

1 Will has £23.7̲5 in his wallet and Marion has £7̲3.50 in hers. How many times larger is the 7 in Marion's amount than the 7̲ in Will's amount?

2 An ice cream parlour kept a record of how many cartons of different ice cream flavours it sold during one week. The results are recorded in the graph below.

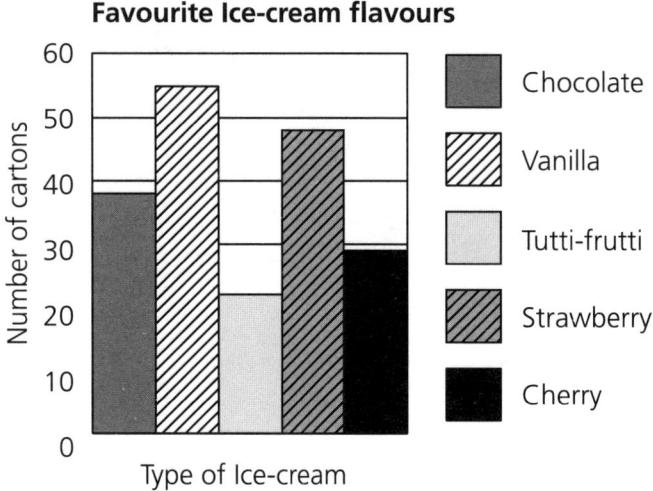

Favourite Ice-cream flavours

How many more cartons of strawberry flavour were sold than cherry flavour?

3 Jim and Margaret flew to Turkey on their holidays. The captain of the plane announced that they were flying at an altitude (height) of thirty-four thousand, seven hundred and twenty-two feet. What is this number written in figures?

4 This machine multiplies by 7 then adds 17. Which number was put in?

⟶ ☐ ⟶ 101

5 Mandeep opens her money box and counts the coins. She calculates she has a total of £6.82. If she has 6 × 2p coins, and the rest are 5p coins, how many 5p coins does her money box contain?

---

6 Which of the following has the smallest value?

A 0.27
B 33 hundredths
C 42%
D 0.207
E 21 hundredths

---

7 Samantha and Andrew conducted a survey on favourite fruits and recorded their results in the table below.

Key:  = 12 votes   = 6 votes

Fruit	Number of votes
Apple	🧺🧺🍑
Pear	🧺
Plum	🍑
Banana	🧺🧺
Peach	🧺🍑

What is the mean number of votes?

---

8 How many times would the triangle shown below fit into the rectangle?

3cm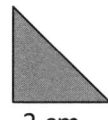
2 cm

3 cm
12 cm

9 Football shirts are priced at £45 for 3. How much money would 7 shirts cost?

10 Which of the following would make a word when rotated through 180°?

A	g	B	t	C	w	D	p	E	e
	o		h		i		o		y
	t		e		n		d		e

11 Angela is allowed to use 600 free minutes on her mobile phone each month. If she uses 137 in the first week and 405 in the second week, how many minutes remain on her balance?

12 The temperature in Frostville was 7°C during the day but fell by 19°C during the night. What was Frostville's temperature during the night?

13 Which of these sets of numbers contains only prime numbers?

A	7	19	27
B	11	21	41
C	9	23	47
D	13	31	53
E	2	17	25

Go straight on to the next page

14 On the treasure island below, pirates like to bury their gold as close to the sea as possible. Which of the following coordinates would be the best place for the pirates to bury their treasure?

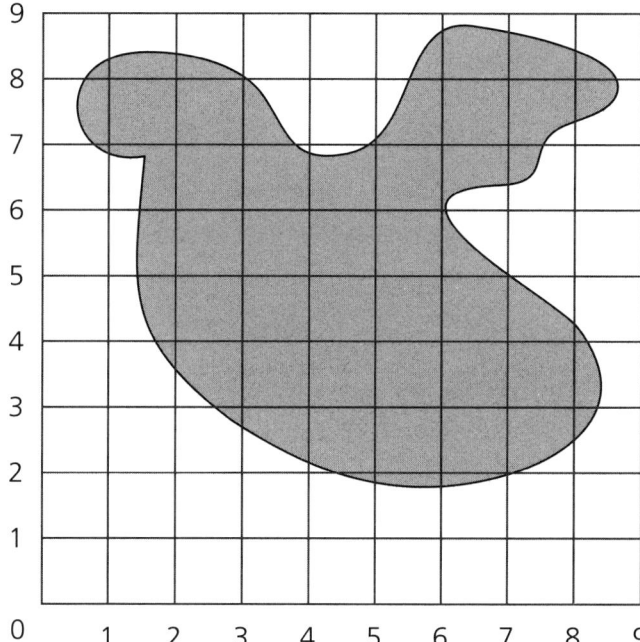

A   (5,4)
B   (6,4)
C   (8,3)
D   (3,5)
E   (5,5)

---

15 Diana is trying to work out her dad's age. He tells her that in 4 years' time he will be 3 times her age at that time. If Diana is 8 years old now, how old is her dad now?

---

16 Which of the following fractions is largest?

A $\frac{3}{7}$

B $\frac{1}{2}$

C $\frac{5}{9}$

D $\frac{7}{11}$

E $\frac{13}{20}$

17 Aaron took part in a sponsored walk for his school. He walked for half an hour at his normal speed. He did not run, neither did he stop until the end. Which distance most likely represents that which he walked in the time?

    A   30 metres
    B   3 kilometres
    C   3000 centimetres
    D   300 metres
    E   30 kilometres

18 A local cake shop bakes 120 cakes every day. Of these, $\frac{1}{6}$ have cherries, $\frac{3}{5}$ have icing and the remainder have raisins. How many have raisins?

19 Arnold posts 3 letters every day for 2 weeks to his friends. If each letter costs 47p to post, how much has he spent after 2 weeks?

20 Candice spends £1,664 each year on maintaining her car and there are 52 weeks in a year. How much does she spend each week?

21 The table below shows how many hours of television some students watched during the week. If the mean for the week was 6 hours, what was the median?

Name	Haley	Kathy	Adrian	Laxman	Walter
Number of hours of TV watched	7	3.5	9	6	?

Go straight on to the next page

22 y = 3x

Which of the following is incorrect?
A   2y = 5x
B   3y = 9x
C   x = $\frac{y}{3}$
D   12x = 4y
E $\frac{y}{x}$ = 3

---

23 A baker delivers bread 5 days a week. If he charges £27.50 each day and he delivers for 9 weeks, how much money does he charge in total?

---

24 The drawing of a courtyard below has a scale of 1:250. How far would it be all the way round the courtyard?

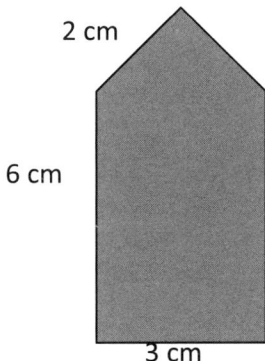

2 cm

6 cm

3 cm

---

25 A box of coloured pencils contains 3 red pencils, 5 blue pencils, 2 green pencils and 4 yellow pencils. If Dominic picks out a pencil at random, what is the chance it will be green?

26 The shape below will make a trapezium with a pair of parallel lines and a pair of equal length lines when point D is added. Where should point D be?

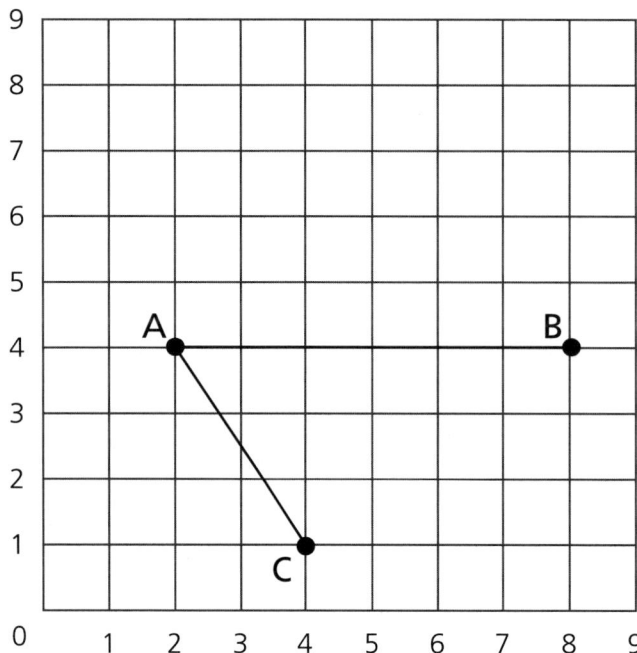

A   (6,1)
B   (8,4)
C   (8,1)
D   (7,2)
E   (5,1)

---

27 Gayle gets some cough medicine for her daughter. Each dose is exactly 2.5ml and the bottle holds 100ml. If Gayle needs to give her daughter the medicine 3 times each day, on which day will it run out?

28

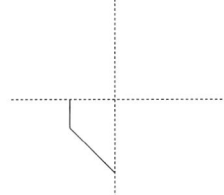

The diagram above shows part of a shape and two of its lines of symmetry.

What is the name of the complete shape?

---

29 Vincent describes the solid shape that he has hidden behind his back. He says it has 6 faces and 8 vertices. Which of the shapes below could it be?

  A   rectangle
  B   cylinder
  C   square based pyramid
  D   triangular prism
  E   cuboid

---

30 Which two shapes do not contain any internal obtuse angles?

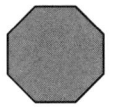  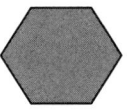 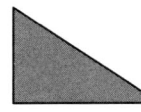 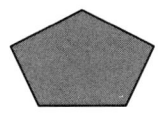

  P   Q   R   S   T

---

31 The headteacher of Saluber Primary School calculates that of the 480 students in the school, 360 eat school meals and the remainder eat packed lunches. Which ratio below shows this information about the types of lunch eaten?

  A   360:400
  B   3:1
  C   120:400
  D   36:40
  E   12:40

Go straight on to the next page

32 What is the missing number?

2	3	5
3	5	7
5	7	?

33 In a restaurant, for every potato the chef cooks, she also cooks 5 carrots. If she cooks a total of 360 vegetables, how many of them are carrots?

34 Kane has to travel 4942km to see his auntie and uncle. After 5 hours on the plane he has travelled $\frac{3}{7}$ of the way. How far has he travelled?

35 Farmer Munton has to weigh his flock of sheep. He weighs 7 of them and their weights are as follows: 60.75kg, 48.2kg, 65.7kg, 53.25kg, 55.32kg, 45.85kg and 48.52kg.

What is the median?

36 In the shape below, two equilateral triangles have been placed back to back.

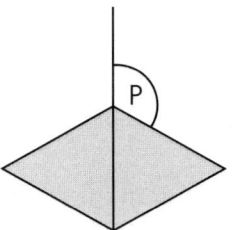

What size is angle P?

37 A publisher prints 450 books. If each book has 132 pages, how many pages are printed in total?

38 Stavros has watched 30 minutes of a 2-hour play. What percentage is this?

39 If $12x - 10 = 4x + 14$, what does x equal?

40 Robert works 5 hours each day for £x an hour and 2 hours' overtime each day at £y an hour. How much money has he earned after 15 days?

41 A local shop offers £5.50 off a shopping bill for any customer spending more than £50. Mrs Marshall wants to buy 3 turkeys costing £21.50 each. How much does she have to pay in total?

42 This is Mr Kensington's garden. What is the total area of grass needed to cover the entire area?

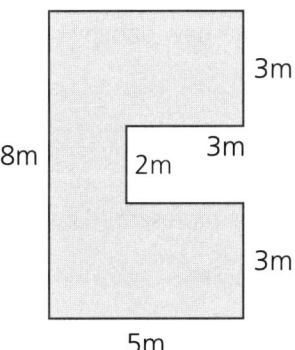

43 450 people were asked to name what transport they used to travel to work each day. The results were recorded in the pie chart below.

How many people used the train?

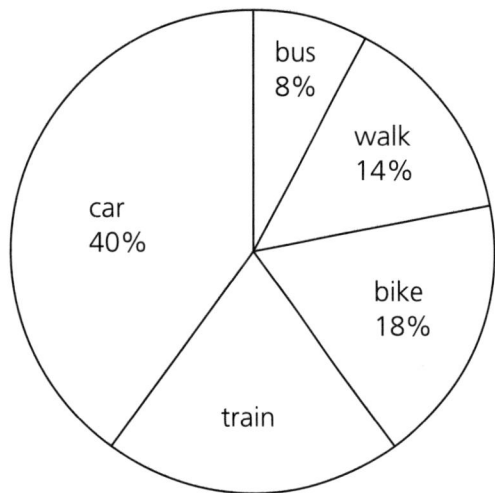

---

44 Tony's Top Toy Shop offers 15% off any toy. If Rick wishes to purchase a new gaming console, which is usually priced at £108, what price does he actually pay?

---

45 A map of Wales is drawn to a scale of 1:400,000. What real distance is represented by 2.5cm on the map?

---

46 What is the mode of the areas of the shapes below?

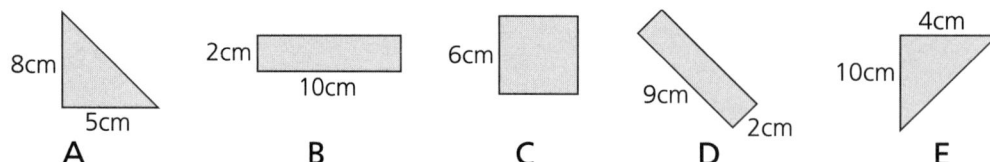

47 How many times will the shape marked K fit inside the shape marked V?

Shape K   Shape V

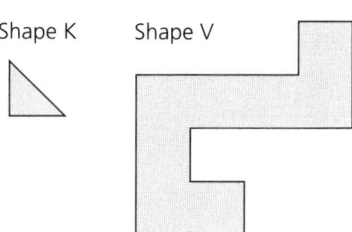

---

48 Victor needs to get out of the maze starting at H and leave by the exit L. Which set of instructions will help him to do this successfully?

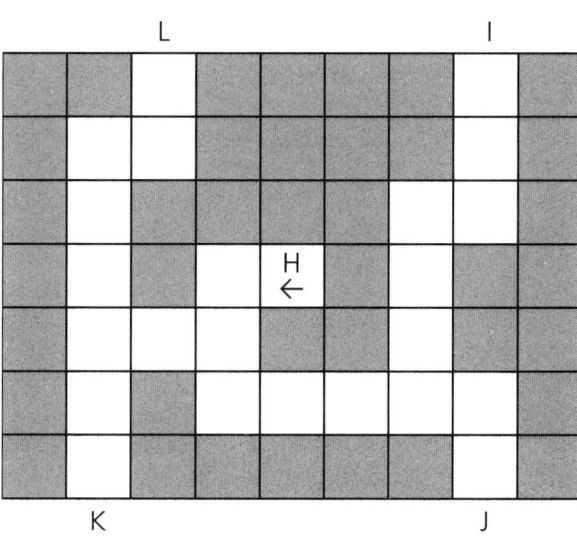

A   Forward 1, Left 90°, Forward 2, Left 90°, Forward 4, Right 90°, Forward 1.
B   Forward 1, Left 90°, Forward 1, Right 90°, Forward 2, Left 90°, Forward 2.
C   Forward 1, Left 90°, Forward 1, Right 90°, Forward 2, Right 90°, Forward 3, Right 90°, Forward 1, Left 90°, Forward 1.
D   Forward 1, Left 90°, Forward 1, Right 90°, Forward 2, Left 90°, Forward 2.
E   Forward 1, Left 90°, Forward 1, Right 90°, Forward 2, Left 90°, Forward 3, Right 90°, Forward 1, Left 90°, Forward 1.

49 Kassim and Kareem are keen runners. They make a note of how many miles they run each week. After 1 week they have both run 60 miles. Kassim then runs h miles per week and Kareem runs j miles per week. Which expression shows how far they have run after 4 more weeks?

50 What is the formula for the area of this shape?

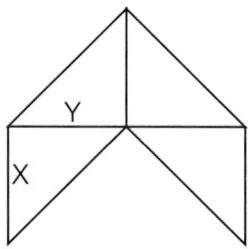

END OF TEST – PLEASE CHECK ALL YOUR ANSWERS

PRACTISE & PASS 11+

MATHS
MULTIPLE CHOICE

PRACTICE PAPER 3

Read the following instructions carefully.

1. Do <u>not</u> begin until you are told to do so.
2. This is a multiple choice test.
3. Answers should be marked on the answer grids provided.
4. Mark your answer in the corresponding answer grid by drawing a firm line clearly in the rectangle next to your answer.
5. If you make a mistake, make sure you rub it out completely before marking a new answer. There should only be one answer marked for each question.
6. You may do any working out on a separate sheet of paper.
7. Make sure you keep your place on the answer grids.
8. Work quickly and carefully. If you cannot do a question, move on to the next one and come back to it later.
9. A calculator may <u>not</u> be used.
10. You will have 50 minutes to complete this test.

1 Wanda is writing an article about a concert. She knows that 23,087 people attended the concert but needs to write this in words. Which answer does this?

- A two thousand three hundred and eighty-seven
- B twenty-three thousand eight hundred and seven
- C two thousand, three thousand and eighty-seven
- D twenty-three thousand and eighty-seven
- E twenty-three thousand and zero and eight-seven

---

2 Mr King conducted a survey to find out how people travelled to work.
He asked 158 people.

Bus	Train	Tram
37	49	26

Mr King has made a mistake. How many people's transport has he forgotten to record?

---

3 Shazad is at the airport. He is told that his 7.30am flight to Dusseldorf has been delayed by 12 hours. What time will it now be leaving?

- A 17.30
- B 07.49
- C 19.30
- D 07.30
- E 07.42

---

4 Which of the following has no lines of reflective symmetry?

- A MnM
- B ¥¤¥
- C ŻĂŻ
- D ΩΨΩ
- E ⊢ ⊣ ∥

Go straight on to the next page

5 Maisy drew a plan of her new bedroom using a scale of 2cm to 7m. If she drew her bedroom as 3cm long on her plan, how long is it in reality?

6 Wesley works at a restaurant. Every night he washes 368 pieces of cutlery. How many pieces of cutlery has he washed after 28 days?

7 Salma played a game with her friends. She told them to think of a number and square it. Which of her friends did <u>not</u> square their number correctly?

Phillip	100
Mercedes	121
Fajer	132
Emma	49
Mike	81

8 What kind of angle is angle Y?

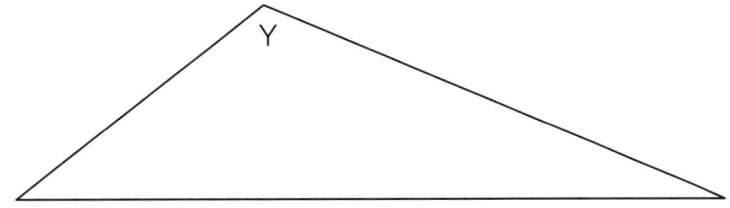

9 Hamish makes 3.6 litres of ice cream each day. If Nick buys 400ml of ice cream from Hamish, what fraction is this of the total?

10 The graph below shows how far children had to travel to get to school. Using this information, which one of the following statements is correct?

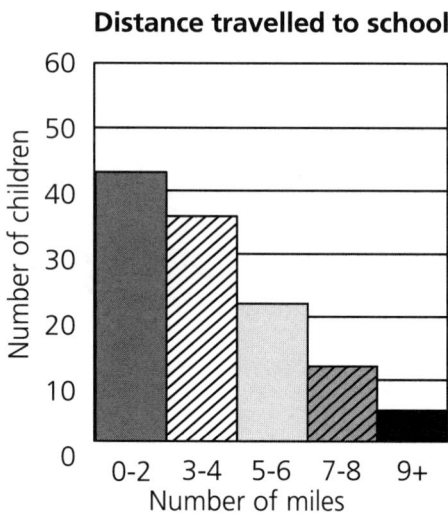

A   Exactly 5 children travel 9 miles to school
B   7–8 children travel 12 miles to school
C   More than 50 children travel fewer than 5 miles to school
D   At least 20 children travel more than 7 miles to school
E   22 children travel 5 miles to school

11 Look at the grid below. What is the missing number?

5	10	20
10	20	40
20	40	?

12 Annabel sold tickets for the school play. The number of tickets she sold in one week is recorded in the table below.

Day	Number of tickets sold
Monday	23
Tuesday	25
Wednesday	31
Thursday	23
Friday	23
Saturday	42
Sunday	32

What is the difference between the mode and the median?

---

13 What size is angle Q in the diagram below?

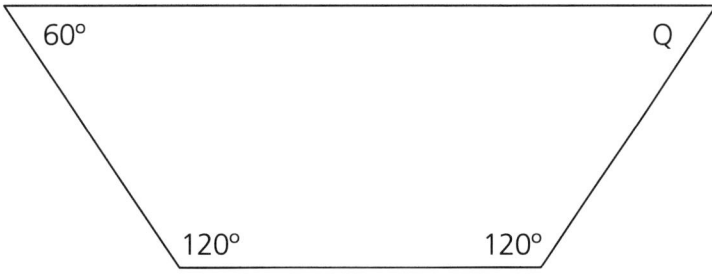

---

14 Look at the number line below. What number is the arrow pointing to?

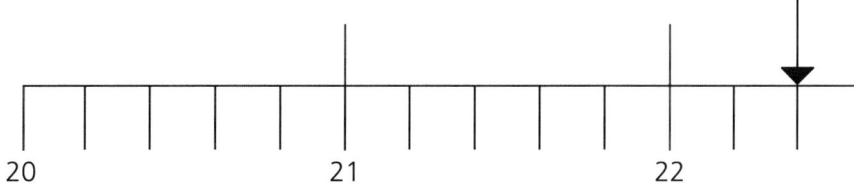

15 Look at the line on the grid below. Which points would mark the ends of a line that would be parallel to this line?

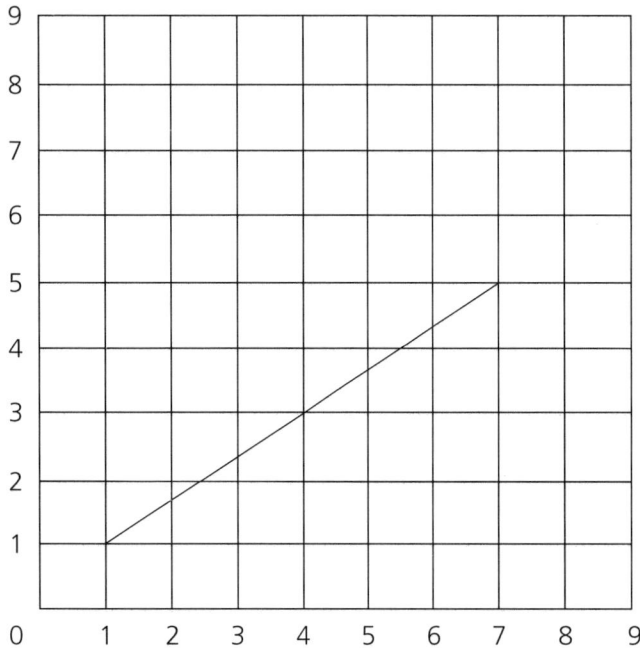

A   (5,4) and (5,7)
B   (6,4) and (8,2)
C   (4,3) and (6,1)
D   (3,5) and (7,5)
E   (1,3) and (8,7)

---

16 On a school trip, the ratio of adults to children is 2:9. If there are 6 adults on the trip, how many students are there?

---

17 At the Charming Sweet Shop, Mr Collins has a board with all the prices of his most popular sweets written on it – see below.

Name of sweet	Price
Bonzos	12p
Cowboy Boots	14p
Fizzy Fizzers	9p
Chewse	7p
Sugar Dips	11p
Phantom Whizzes	22p

Claire buys 3 Bonzos, 7 Sugar Dips and 3 Phantom Whizzes. How much change does she receive from a £2 coin?

18 How many of the following shapes contain a right angle?

   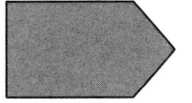 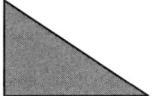

---

19 What are the coordinates of points P, Q and R in that order?

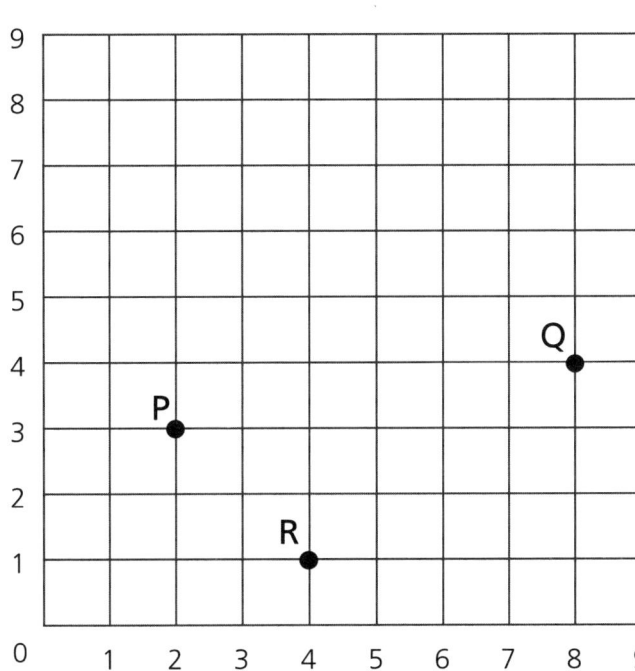

A	(2,3)	(4,1)	(8,4)
B	(2,3)	(8,4)	(4,1)
C	(8,4)	(4,1)	(2,3)
D	(3,2)	(8,4)	(4,1)
E	(2,3)	(4,8)	(4,1)

---

20 Bob says that each row of numbers is made by doubling the first number to get the second and then subtracting 9 to get the third. Which row of numbers does not do this?

A	19	38	29
B	23	46	37
C	42	84	75
D	27	54	44
E	22	44	35

Go straight on to the next page

21 In a survey of 84 people, every 7th person had a pet. How many people had a pet?

A $84 - 7$
B $84 + 7$
C 84×7
D 84×0.7
E $84 \times \frac{1}{7}$

22 What size is angle T?

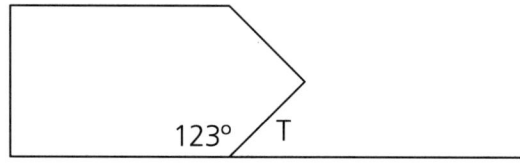

23 A walker leaves point H and travels 3km east and then 2km north. What are the coordinates of the point where he finishes his walk?

Key: 1 square = 1km

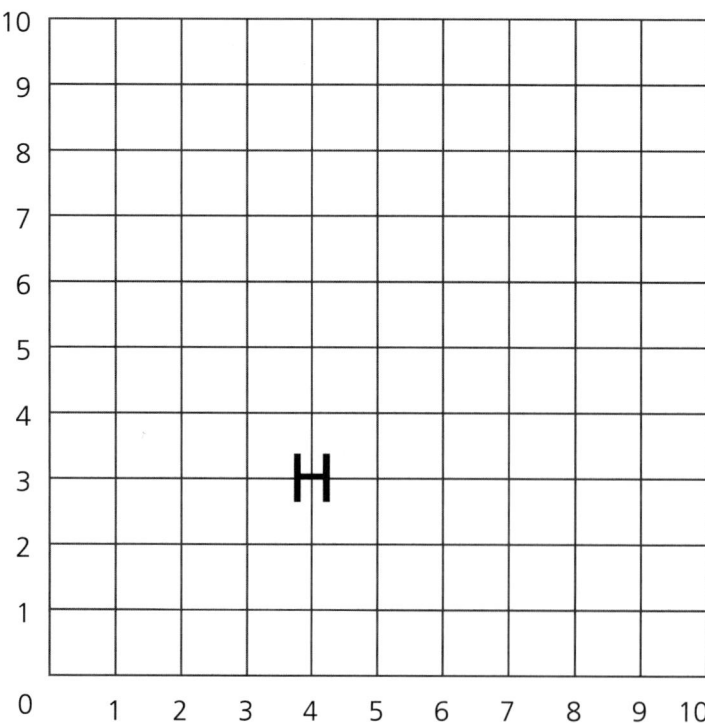

24 Year 6 collected information about their favourite pizza topping.

Topping	Number of votes
Pepperoni	13
Mushroom	24
Cheese	33
Chicken	21
Tuna	11
Tomato	?

The mean is 22. How many people voted for tomato?

25 Katie receives £3.60 pocket money each week but her elder sister June receives 2.5 times as much. How much money does June receive over a 12-week period?

26 A local hardware shop keeps screws in boxes of 40. If there are 930 screws, how many boxes are needed to contain them all?

27 The game below is played by spinning an arrow and watching which number it lands on.

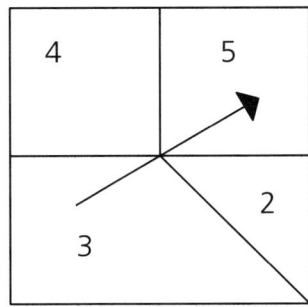

What is the probability it will land on an odd number?

28 5 years ago Imran was twice his sister's age then. Imran is now 19. How old is his sister now?

Go straight on to the next page

29 The table below shows the times (in seconds) sprinters took to run the 100m race.

Name	Khan	Rod	Ian	Vince	Louis	Ben	Jack	Will
Time	10.03	10.31	10.09	10.35	10.51	10.44	10.28	10.8

What is the range of their times?

---

30 Which of the amounts below is the largest?

A   0.6
B $\frac{16}{25}$
C   62%
D   6.8%
E   0.09

---

31 In a shopping centre there are 3 times as many clothes shops as there are food shops. If there are 76 shops in total, how many are clothes shops?

---

32 How many of the shapes below have <u>both</u> reflective and rotational symmetry?

    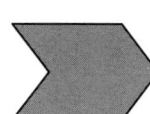

33 Lulu wants to buy a new computer. It costs £300 but she has to borrow the money and pay an extra 10% of the original price. If she pays it back over 15 weeks, how much must she pay back each week?

34 The area of the shaded rectangle is 25cm². What is the area of all 8 rectangles when combined together?

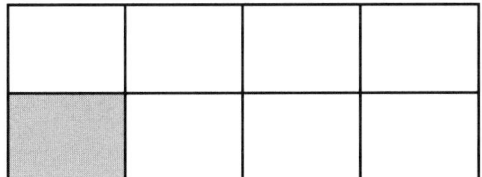

35 The area of a rectangle is 28cm². What could the perimeter be?

    A   20cm
    B   21cm
    C   22cm
    D   23cm
    E   24cm

36 This pie chart shows the different proportions of colours of dresses in a shop.

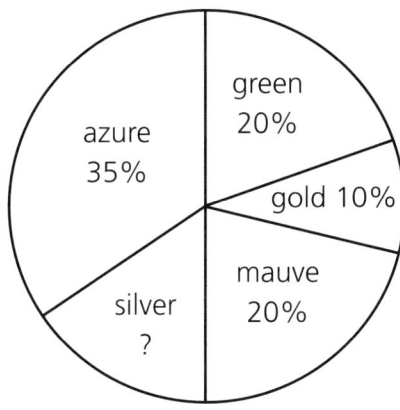

If there are 16 gold dresses, how many silver dresses are there?

37 A map of Luxembourg is drawn to a scale of 1:550,000. What is the real distance represented by 3cm?

---

38 Which of the following is not equivalent?

    A   0.32
    B   32%
    C $\frac{32}{100}$
    D $\frac{8}{25}$
    E   3.2

---

39 If $4x + 3y = 2z$, which of the following is correct?

    A $4y + 2x = 2z$
    B $3x + y = z$
    C $8x + 6y = 4z$
    D $3x + 4y = 2z$
    E $3z - (6y + 3x)$

---

40 A rainwater barrel, which holds 18 litres of water, loses 300ml of water each day due to a leak. How much water will the barrel hold after 12 days?

41 A museum records visitor numbers over several hours. In the first hour 78 people entered. In the second hour, 43 people left and 29 people entered. In the third hour 54 people entered and 32 people left. In the final hour 62 people entered and 21 people left.

How many people were then in the museum after 4 hours?

---

42 The table below shows how much objects would weigh on the planet Mars. The scientists have not completed the table. Which value would complete it?

	Earth weight	Mars weight
1	1 pound	0.38 pound
2	2 pounds	0.76 pound
3	3 pounds	?
4	4 pounds	1.52 pounds

---

43 Toby's favourite magazine costs £3.99 and comes out monthly. How much will it cost him to buy the magazine for half a year?

---

44 A shop sells tea and coffee. If 3 boxes of coffee have the same value as 5 boxes of tea, which of the following statements is incorrect?

- A   6 boxes of coffee = 12 boxes of tea
- B   9 boxes of coffee = 15 boxes of tea
- C   20 boxes of tea = 12 boxes of coffee
- D   6 boxes of coffee weigh less than 15 boxes of tea
- E   25 boxes of tea = 15 boxes of coffee

Go straight on to the next page

45 A zookeeper feeds a zebra 5kg of apples at 48p per kg, 12kg of dried fruits at £1.10 per kg, 8kg of hay at 30p per kg and 2kg of vitamins at £3.25 per kg. What is the total cost for 1 day?

---

46 Paulo measures his desk. It is 1m 20cm long. Which of the measurements below is closest to this?

    A   40 inches
    B   44 inches
    C   48 inches
    D   50 inches
    E   53 inches

---

47 Which answer has the smallest value?

    A $\frac{1}{5}$ of 65
    B   10% of 150
    C   0.5 × 140
    D   12
    E $\frac{4}{8}$ of 28

---

48 In a sandwich shop Sue varies her menu each day of the week. She sells x chicken sandwiches each Monday, Wednesday and Friday. She also sells y salad sandwiches each Tuesday and Thursday. How many sandwiches has she sold after 5 weeks?

Go straight on to the next page

49 Which of the following shapes does not contain at least two equally sized angles?

 A   Isosceles triangle
 B   Regular pentagon
 C   Kite
 D   Regular hexagon
 E   Scalene triangle

---

50 Victor needs to get out of the maze starting at H and leaving by the exit L. Which set of instructions will help him to do this successfully?

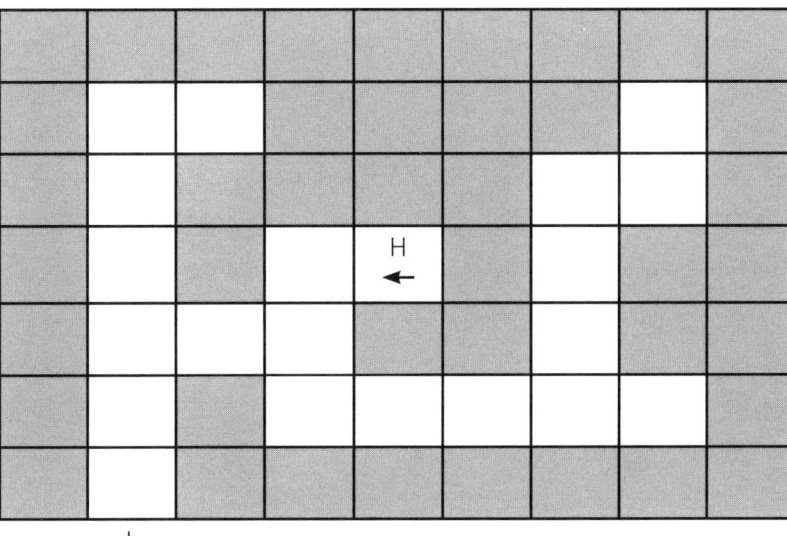

 A   Forward 1, Left 90°, Forward 2, Left 90°, Forward 4, Right 90°, Forward 1.

 B   Forward 2, Left 90°, Forward 1, Right 90°, Forward 3, Left 90°, Forward 2.

 C   Forward 1, Left 90°, Forward 1, Right 90°, Forward 2, Right 90°, Forward 3, Right 90°, Forward 1, Left 90°, Forward 1.

 D   Forward 1, Left 90°, Forward 1, Right 90°, Forward 2, Left 90°, Forward 2.

 E   Forward 1, Left 90°, Forward 1, Right 90°, Forward 2, Left 90°, Forward 3, Right 90°, Forward 1, Left 90°, Forward 1.

PRACTISE & PASS 11+

MATHS
MULTIPLE CHOICE

PRACTICE PAPER 4

Read the following instructions carefully.

1. Do not begin until you are told to do so.
2. This is a multiple choice test.
3. Answers should be marked on the answer grids provided.
4. Mark your answer in the corresponding answer grid by drawing a firm line clearly in the rectangle next to your answer.
5. If you make a mistake, make sure you rub it out completely before marking a new answer. There should only be one answer marked for each question.
6. You may do any working out on a separate sheet of paper.
7. Make sure you keep your place on the answer grids.
8. Work quickly and carefully. If you cannot do a question, move on to the next one and come back to it later.
9. A calculator may not be used.
10. You will have 50 minutes to complete this test.

1 An internet website received 30,073 visitors in 2010 and 33,068 visitors in 2011. How many more people visited it in 2011?

2 At a breakfast club in Sunny Primary School, the children record how many cartons of juice they drink each morning. Their results are shown below:

Day	Cartons drunk
Monday	
Tuesday	
Wednesday	
Thursday	
Friday	

How many cartons were drunk on Wednesday?

3 Amy needs 5 litres of water to fill her goldfish bowl. Which of the following containers would be closest to holding that amount?

A   egg cup
B   mug
C   bucket
D   kettle
E   soup spoon

4 In 2007 a local park group was started with 14 members. In 2008 the number of members doubled and in 2009 there were half the number of members again as there had been in 2008. In 2010 the number of members trebled. How many members were there in 2010?

5 Colin takes his daughter to school every third day; his friend Rupert takes his son to the same school but every second day. Sometimes they meet up. If they both take their children to school on Monday, when is the next day they both take their children to school?

---

6 Stavros went to his local supermarket. His bill came to £37.04 but he had two coupons that reduced his bill by 75p each. What is his new bill?

---

7 The table below shows the number of people who visited the train museum each year.

Year	2005	2006	2007	2008	2009	2010
Number of people visiting	2,033	1,057	3,652	2,823	3,705	?

If a total of 16,000 people visited, how many visited the museum in 2010?

---

8 A group of scouts is building a new hut. Ellie notices that the main supports are each 4.2m long each but only 3.4m can be seen above ground once they have been erected. How much of each support is below ground?

Go straight on to the next page

9 Wanda is writing her assignment. She writes 346 words for each page and writes a total of 78 pages. How many words has she written in total?

10 Which of the following sets of numbers are all multiples of either 3 or 7?

  A   6, 10, 21
  B   9, 14, 27
  C   10, 21, 28
  D   14, 15, 25
  E   14, 18, 26

11 Which of the shapes below has rotational symmetry of order three?

A  B 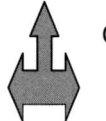 C  D 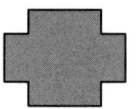 E

12 Frank spent £3.51 on 13 toy dinosaurs. He sold them for a total of £3.77 so how much profit did he make on each?

13 Patrice has 2 × 50p pieces, 3 × 20p pieces and a 5p piece. Her friend George has 4 × £1 coins, 5 × 10p pieces and 6 × 2p pieces. How much money do they have all together?

14 This machine adds 49 then reduces the total by 20%.

Which number comes out?

15 Point X (1.2, 1.5) is reflected through the line drawn from point A at (1.2, 1.2) and point B at (1.6, 1.6). Where will the new coordinates of X be?

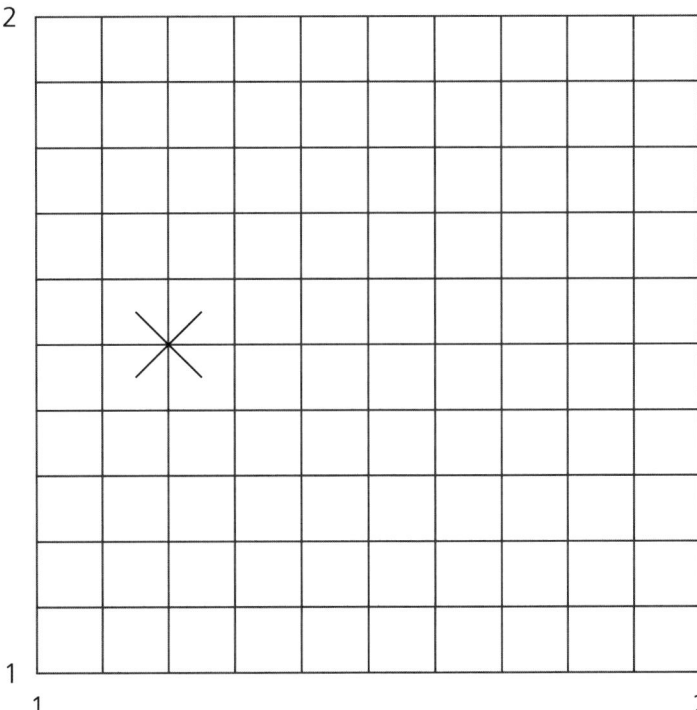

16 A school needs to file all the pupil folders. If each filing cabinet can hold 45 folders and there are 360 folders in all, how many filing cabinets are needed to file them all?

Go straight on to the next page

17 Football shirts in a local sports shop are sold at £168 for 4. How much would 3 shirts cost?

18 Jenny drew a plan of her local park using a scale of 3cm to 7m. On the plan the pond is 12cm long; what is its real length?

19 A newspaper boy wants to deliver papers to all of the houses on an estate. He does not want to use a street more than once but he can pass over the same street corners more than once. On which estate is this possible?

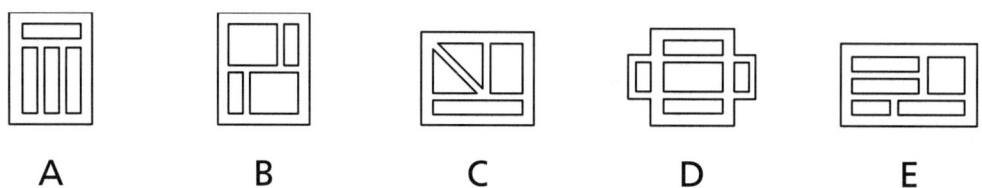

20

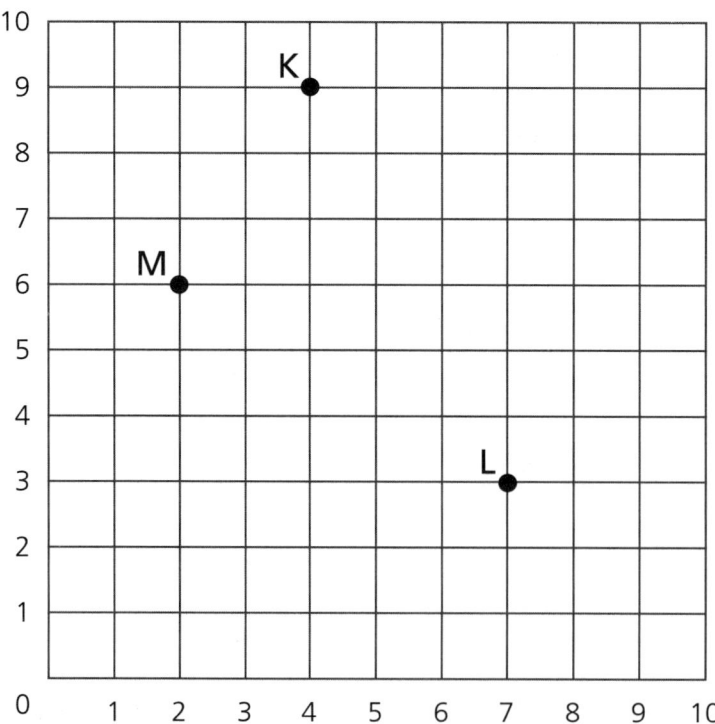

What are the coordinates of the point K?

21 Which of the solid shapes below has 6 edges and 4 faces?

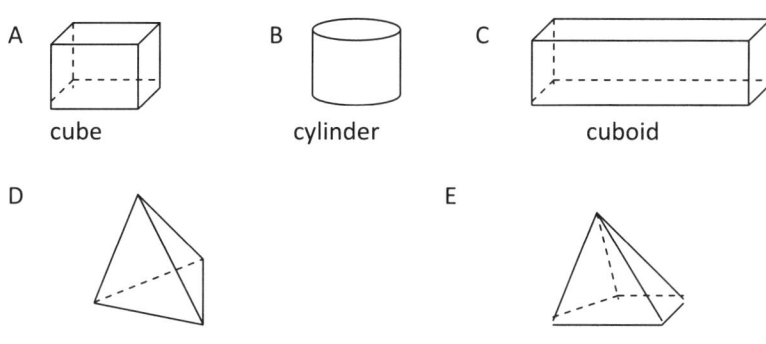

A cube B cylinder C cuboid D triangular based pyramid E square based pyramid

22 A group of walkers set out on a walk at 9am and finished at 3pm. The graph below shows how many miles they walked during each hour between those times. Between which hours did the walkers stop for lunch?

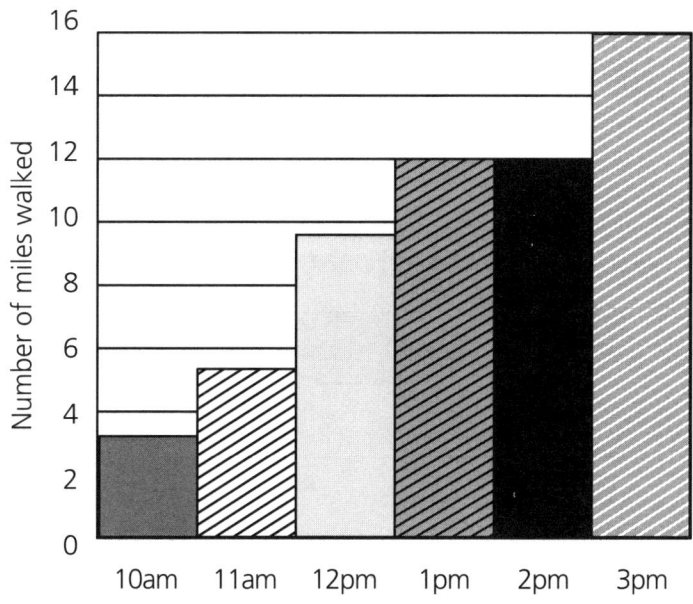

23 A number is multiplied by itself, then it is trebled and the answer is 75.
What was the initial number?

Go straight on to the next page

24 Look at the number line below. Which number does the arrow point to?

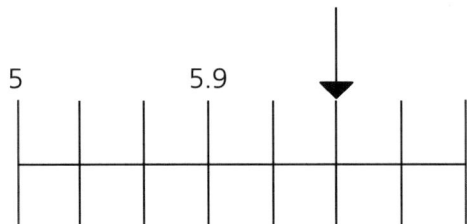

---

25 Of 120 students in a year group, $\frac{5}{6}$ attend every day at school. How many students is this?

---

26 How many matchsticks are needed to make the next shape in this sequence?

---

27 Which of these shapes have reflective symmetry?

P    Q    R    S 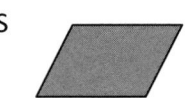   T

---

28 In a bag of mixed coins there are 4 × 10p coins, 5 × 5p coins, 3 × 20p coins and 8 × 50p coins. What is the probability that a 10p coin will be picked out?

---

29 Look at the grid below. Which number is missing?

?	54	18
54	18	6
18	6	2

30 Miranda designs sets for bedrooms. In each set she has 3 colours of sheets, 2 types of pillows and 5 patterns of curtains. How many different bedroom sets can she make?

31

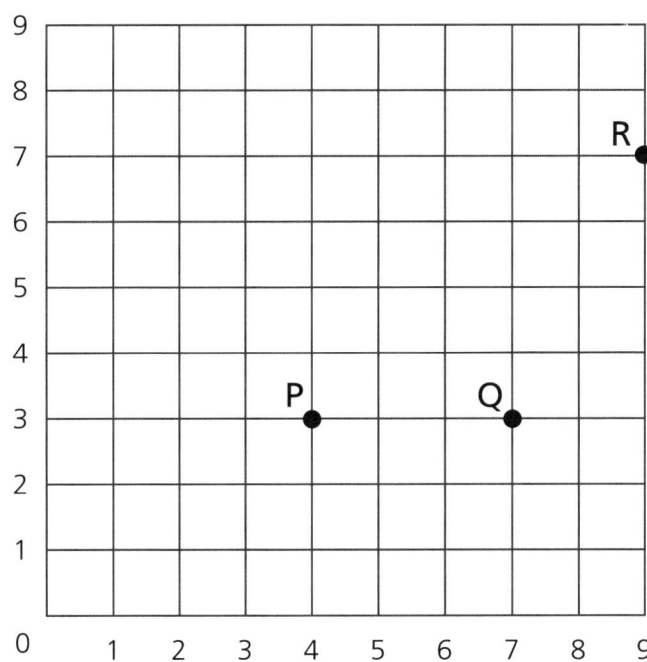

The points P, Q and R are the corners of a parallelogram. What are the coordinates of the missing point which would complete the corners of the shape?

A   (7,6)
B   (6,6)
C   (5,7)
D   (6,7)
E   (6,8)

---

32 Clarence looked at the letters in his name. What percentage of them are vowels?

---

33 Haroula was x years old 5 years ago. How old will she be in 4 years' time?

Go straight on to the next page

34 Farouq needs a stick 1 metre high for his plants to grow up. Which of the following sticks is closest to that length?

A 200cm
B 99cm
C 101cm
D 99.8cm
E 100.01cm

35 Cheryl used the decision tree below to sort some jewellery she found.

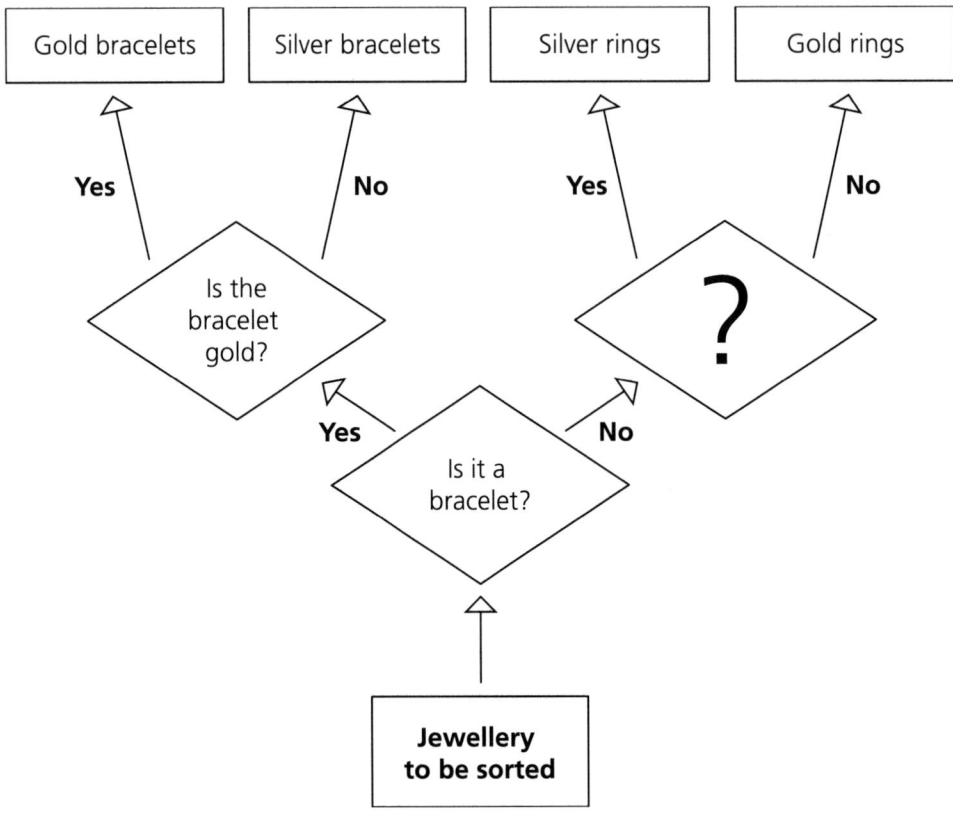

What is missing from the empty shape?

A Gold rings
B Silver rings
C Is the ring gold?
D Is the ring silver?
E Is it a ring?

36 Veronica returned from her holiday with some souvenirs. She bought some sunglasses for €15, and a hat for €8. She calculates that the sunglasses cost £12 and the hat cost £6.40. How much would a shirt for €7 cost in pounds?

---

37 Wasim measured his school desk as 30 inches long. Which of these measurements is closest to this?

A   60cm
B   65cm
C   70cm
D   75cm
E   80cm

---

38 A lucky dip party game has a bag containing 7 bracelets, 5 bubble makers, 6 party hats and 2 bouncy balls.

If a gift is picked at random, in which <u>one</u> of the following are <u>both</u> statements true?

A   You have a better than even chance of picking a bracelet.
      You have an even chance of picking a party hat.

B   You are certain to pick a gift.
      You have a better than even chance of picking a bubble maker.

C   You are certain to pick a gift.
      You are unlikely to pick a bracelet.

D   You are certain to pick a gift.
      You are likely to pick a party hat.

E   You are certain to pick a gift.
      You are likely to pick a bracelet.

39 Lee used his calculator to work out an answer of 8.2539. However he only needs to know it to 2 decimal places. Which answer gives this?

40 If 5x + 11 = 44 − 6x, what is x?

41 Wendy wishes to have a new carpet fitted in her lounge. The carpet she wishes to buy costs £5.99 per square metre. How much will it cost her in total? A plan of her lounge is shown below.

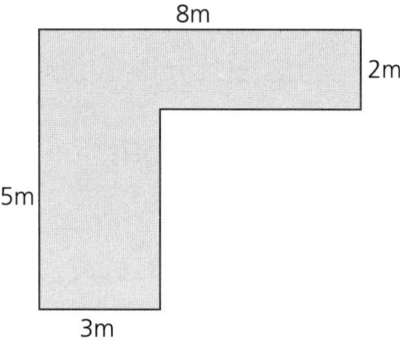

42 What is the area of the shape below?

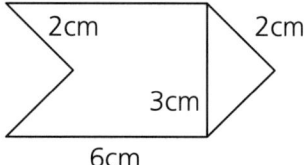

43 Which of the following shows a factor of 100, a prime number and a multiple of 3 in that order?

	A	B	C	D	E
A	25	17	35
B	20	19	303
C	4	2	38
D	200	7	33
E	50	12	120

44 Kassim needs to direct his electronic car through the maze from point H to point E. Which set of directions will do this?

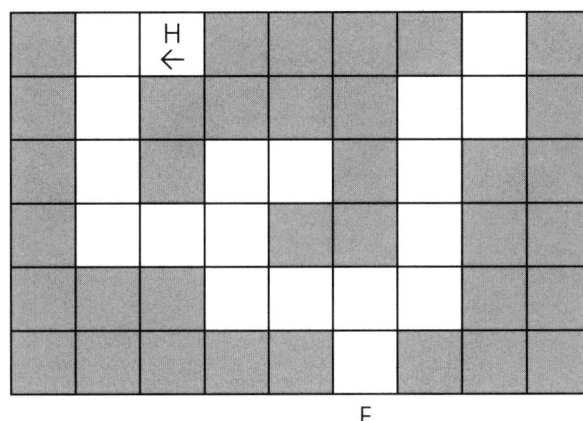

A   Forward 1, Left 90°, Forward 2, Right 90°, Forward 2, Right 90°, Forward 2, Right 90°, Forward 1.

B   Forward 1, Left 90°, Forward 3, Left 90°, Forward 2, Left 90°, Forward 1, Left 90°, Forward 2, Left 90°, Forward 1.

C   Forward 1, Left 90°, Forward 3, Left 90°, Forward 2, Right 90°, Forward 1, Left 90°, Forward 2, Right 90°, Forward 1.

D   Forward 1, Left 90°, Forward 3, Left 90°, Forward 2, Right 90°, Forward 2, Left 90°, Forward 2, Right 90°, Forward 1.

E   Forward 1, Left 90°, Forward 4, Left 90°, Forward 2, Right 90°, Forward 2, Left 90°, Forward 2, Right 90°, Forward 1.

45 Which of the following is a multiple of 3, 5 and 6?

A 24
B 32
C 40
D 30
E 15

---

46 In the diagram below, each square represents 2cm². What is the combined area of the 2 shapes below?

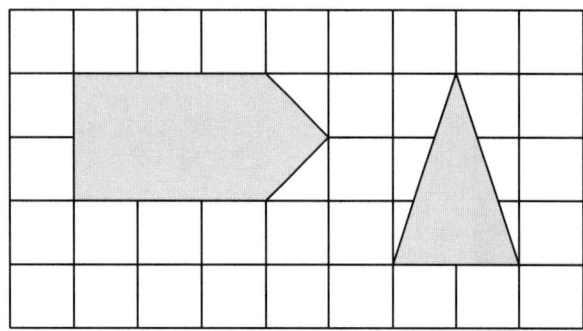

---

47 Alan wants to pack boxes of computer consoles into one larger box. How many of the smaller console boxes can he fit into the larger box?

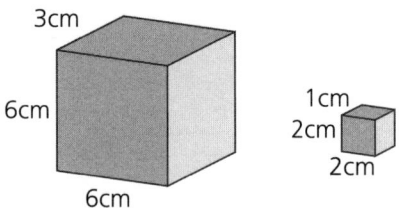

---

48 Julian collects stamps. The number he collected each day for a week is recorded in the table below.

Day	Number of stamps
Monday	17
Tuesday	11
Wednesday	23
Thursday	14
Friday	?

If the range of Julian's collection is 15 how many stamps did he collect on Friday?

49 What is the area of the shape below?

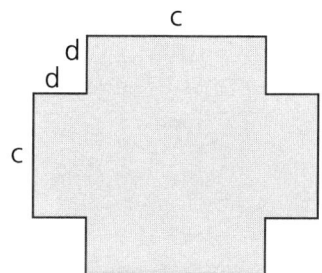

50 The pie chart below shows which parts of a playground children enjoyed using most.

15 children liked the slide. How many liked the roundabout?

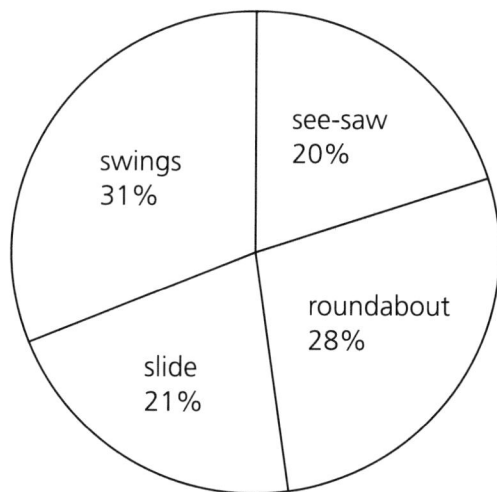

END OF TEST - PLEASE CHECK ALL YOUR ANSWERS

PRACTISE & PASS 11+

MATHS
ANSWERS AND ADVICE FOR PARENTS

Read this <u>before</u> the student starts taking any of the practice test papers.

Contents

Timings and rules for Maths practice papers	3
Suggested mock test schedule	3
Marking the tests: correct answers and answer explanations	5
Practice paper 1	6
Practice paper 2	7
Practice paper 3	8
Practice paper 4	9
How to improve scores	10
Further help	27

© Peter Williams and Trotman Publishing, 2015

The right of Peter Williams to be identified as the author of this work has been asserted by him in accordance with the Copyright, Designs and Patents Act, 1988.

All rights reserved. No part of this publication may be transmitted in any form or by any means, or stored in a retrieval system without prior written permission from the publisher.

First published 2015 by Trotman Publishing, a division of Crimson Publishing Ltd, 19–21c Charles Street, Bath BA1 1HX.

ISBN 978 1 84455 428 7

A catalogue record for this book is available from the British Library.

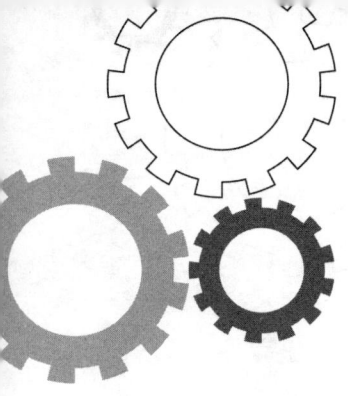
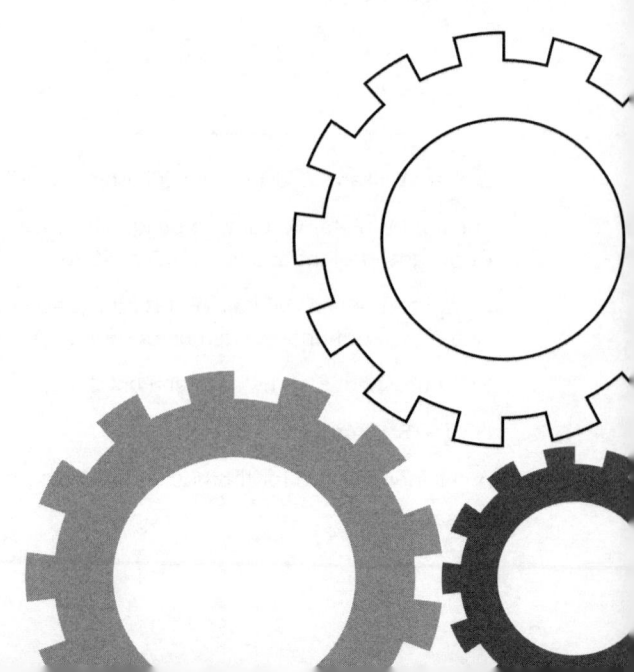

TIMINGS AND RULES FOR MATHS PRACTICE PAPERS

SETTING THE TEST

- Allow 50 minutes for the entire test.
- Do not read or explain any terms or words to the student.
- Do not explain how to work out any of the problems.
- A calculator may _not_ be used.
- Time the test precisely and stop the student when the allotted time is over.
- Students may be informed when they are halfway through the allotted time and when there are five minutes remaining.

GUIDANCE FOR TESTING

- Do explain to students before the test that there will be some very difficult questions and they could appear at any point in the test. Tell students to mark these on the paper and come back to them. Tell them not to waste time fretting about really tough questions, just to get on and answer the questions they know how to answer!
- Do tell students to write down workings for each question where possible. These will prove invaluable when checking at the end.
- Get students to check they have marked an answer in each answer grid – often students forget to do this for each question or mark them in the wrong order or even mark two on one grid and none on the next.

SUGGESTED MOCK TEST SCHEDULE

If you want the student to take the practice papers in a mock test format, then you can follow the suggestions below on how to do this. All exams are different in nature so the tests that are set, the order in which papers are given and which question styles are included can vary. If the student has worked through _Practise & Pass 11+ Level One: Discover Maths_ and _Practise & Pass 11+ Level Two: Develop Maths_ they will be familiar with the most common question styles.

SET UP

- Set up a clear desk. Have a pencil, rubber and spare blank paper set out.
- Make sure a simple, analogue clock is easily visible.
- Follow all rules and timings precisely (see above).
- Do not give any extra help even if you can see that the student is making a mistake.
- If the student requires a bathroom break during a paper, let them go but explain that no extra time will be given.
- Try to get the student to use the full amount of time – they will not be allowed to leave the room early in the actual exam.

INCLUDING OTHER TESTS

If you want to replicate a true exam experience give the student other test types to do, using the other titles in the *Practise & Pass 11+ Level Three* series. Follow the suggested times given for each type of test and give the student a 10 minute break to have a quick drink and use the bathroom after completing each test.

Note: It is rare for students to have to take papers in all areas so it is important for parents to find out which papers are relevant and have the student take only those.

Once you know which papers your child needs to sit then set out a schedule as follows.

- Test 1 – 50 minutes
- Break – 10 minutes
- Test 2 – 50 minutes
- Break – 10 minutes
- Test 3 – 50 minutes

Please note that non-verbal reasoning has different timings to English, maths and verbal reasoning so take account of this when planning your 'mock' day for your child.

WRITING PAPER

If you want to set the writing paper as part of your mock English test, choose just one title for your child to do. Do not give them a choice of titles unless the school for which you are preparing specifically does this. If you decide to give your child more than one set of mock exams, try choosing a different type of writing title so that they have experience of creative writing and non-fiction styles.

Note: Different schools allocate different time limits for the writing paper (if they are setting one), from 20 minutes to 45 minutes. You should check with the school how much time will be allowed but if no time is given, or you are unable to find out, allow the student 30 minutes to sit the writing paper.

MARKING THE TESTS: CORRECT ANSWERS AND ANSWER EXPLANATIONS

The following pages contain the correct answers for practice papers 1, 2, 3 and 4. If a student has answered incorrectly go through the explanation with them to ensure they understand where they went wrong. If they are still struggling, go back to the relevant sections of *Practise & Pass 11+ Level One: Discover Maths* and *Practise & Pass 11+ Level Two: Develop Maths* and practise those types of question again. You can also refer to the section on how to improve scores (p.10) for tips on further practice.

When marking the tests parents should remember that there are no half marks – the answer should be marked either correct or incorrect. Any workings out on scrap paper should not be marked. If the student has written the correct answer on a piece of working out paper but marked the incorrect letter on the corresponding grid answer sheet, the answer is incorrect.

It is vital that students practise how to mark the correct answer on the multiple choice grids so do not consider any working out on scrap paper.

PRACTICE PAPER 1

1. 300
2. 6 to 9
3. 560
4. 27%
5. £0.78
6. 37.5cm
7. 156
8. 1,817
9. D
10. (20, 15)
11. 75
12. 27cm^2
13. 108
14. 2
15. 23.35cm
16. E
17. x + 8 years
18. 56
19. £66
20. £6.09
21. 1.6km
22. B
23. 56
24. 6
25. £3.85
26. 85%
27. £12.95
28. 4
29. 13.5cm
30. 175g
31. P (2,8) Q (4,3) R (9,7)
32. s + 12t
33. 57
34. 57cm^2
35. x = 9
36. 48
37. C
38. C
39. E
40. £9.34
41. trapezium
42. C
43. 16
44. 3km
45. E
46. 10.5cm^2
47. 45°
48. B
49. D
50. C

PRACTICE PAPER 2

1. 100
2. 19
3. 34,722
4. 12
5. 134
6. D
7. 18
8. 12
9. £105
10. E
11. 58
12. -12°C
13. D
14. C
15. 32
16. E
17. B
18. 28
19. £19.74
20. £32
21. 6
22. A
23. £1,237.50
24. 47.5m
25. $\frac{1}{7}$
26. A
27. 14th
28. hexagon
29. E
30. Q and S
31. B
32. 11
33. 300
34. 2,118km
35. 53.25kg
36. 120°
37. 59,400
38. 25%
39. x = 3
40. 75x + 30y
41. £59.00
42. 34m²
43. 90
44. £91.80
45. 10km
46. 20cm²
47. 16
48. C
49. 4j + 4h + 60
50. 4(XY/2)

PRACTICE PAPER 3

1. D
2. 46
3. C
4. C
5. 10.5m
6. 10,304
7. Fajer
8. obtuse
9. $\frac{1}{9}$
10. C
11. 80
12. 2
13. 60°
14. 22.4
15. E
16. 27
17. 21p
18. 3
19. B
20. D
21. E
22. 57°
23. (7,5)
24. 30
25. £108
26. 24
27. $\frac{5}{8}$
28. 12
29. 0.77
30. B
31. 57
32. 2
33. £22
34. 200cm^2
35. C
36. 24
37. 16.5km
38. E
39. C
40. 14.4 litres
41. 127
42. 1.14 pounds
43. £23.94
44. A
45. £24.50
46. C
47. D
48. 15x + 10y
49. E
50. D

PRACTICE PAPER 4

1. 2,995
2. 21 to 24
3. C
4. 126
5. Tuesday
6. £35.54
7. 2,730
8. 0.8m
9. 26,988
10. B
11. D
12. 2p
13. £6.27
14. 52
15. (1.5, 1.2)
16. 8
17. £126
18. 28m
19. D
20. (4,9)
21. D
22. 1 and 2
23. 5
24. 6.5
25. 100
26. 17
27. Q and R
28. 20%
29. 162
30. 30
31. D
32. 37.5%
33. x + 5 + 4
34. E
35. D
36. £5.60
37. D
38. C
39. 8.25
40. x = 3
41. £149.75
42. $18cm^2$
43. B
44. C
45. D
46. $20cm^2$
47. 27
48. 8
49. $c^2 + 4(cd)$
50. 20

HOW TO IMPROVE SCORES

Students scoring 35 out of 50 or fewer in each paper may require further practice. There are several ways students can improve upon their initial scores. Here are some more help and tips to help them achieve a better score.

TIMINGS

Often students either struggle to complete all the questions in the time, or they race through and finish with a lot of time to spare. Neither of these situations is ideal.

If your child was not able to finish all the questions you need to find out why. Ask them to point out any difficult questions that they encountered in the paper – this will be where they have lost time. Encourage them to practise these questions but also encourage them to 'skip' these questions, complete the paper and then return to them at the end. In this way your child will get to see all of the questions and spend enough time on those questions they find easier before tackling the more difficult ones.

Encourage them to underline key words in questions and to read questions carefully. Also encourage students to think about whether or not their answers are reasonable. The more they make notes and write things down, the less likely they are to miss vital information.

FURTHER TIPS

- Do tell students to write down workings for each question where possible. These will prove invaluable when checking at the end.
- Get students to check they have marked an answer in each answer grid – often students forget to do this for each question or mark them in the wrong order or even mark two on one grid and none on the next.

FURTHER PRACTICE

It's well worth going over any questions your child got wrong and explaining to them how to get the right answer. If you'd like more questions of a certain type to practise or if you're unsure of the best way to explain a particular question, use this breakdown of where to find different question types in the first two titles in the Practise and Pass series, *Practise & Pass 11+ Level One: Discover Maths* and *Practise & Pass 11+ Level Two: Develop Maths*. That way you can find out how best to explain the questions to them and also give your child lots more practice to help them improve.

Any question types which are not included in *Practise & Pass 11+ Level One: Discover Maths* and *Practise & Pass 11+ Level Two: Develop Maths* are explained at the end along with some tips on how to revise for these types of questions.

Practice paper 1: question types and further practice references

Question	Answer	Type of question	*Practise & Pass 11+ Level One: Discover Maths* lessons to refer to for further practice	*Practise & Pass 11+ Level Two: Develop Maths* lessons to refer to for further practice	Other titles in the *Practise & Pass 11+* series to refer to
1.	300	Place value	Lesson 1		
2.	6 to 9	Handling data		Lesson 12	
3.	560	Fraction of a whole number	Lesson 2	Lesson 2	
4.	27%	Handling data/using subtraction		Lessons 1 and 12	
5.	£0.78	Simple division (see Further help p. 28)			
6.	37.5cm	Division/metric measures	Page 124 (metric measures)		
7.	156	Averages/ranges	Lesson 14	Lesson 14	
8.	1,817	Long multiplication		Lesson 13	
9.	D	Symmetry			Shape builder in *Practise & Pass 11+ Level One: Discover Non-verbal Reasoning* pages 16 and 76
10.	(20, 15)	Coordinates (see Further help p. 28)			
11.	75	Finding whole numbers from a fraction	Lesson 3	Lesson 3	
12.	27cm^2	Perimeter	Lesson 10		
13.	108	Number machines (see Further help p. 29)			

14.	2	Logic problems			*Practise & Pass 11+ Level Two: Develop Verbal Reasoning* lesson 10
15.	23.35cm	Rounding with decimals		Lesson 5	
16.	E	Estimating length (see Further help p. 30)			
17.	x + 8 years	Algebraic formulae (see Further help p. 28)			
18.	56	Fraction of a whole number	Lesson 2	Lesson 2	
19.	£66	Ratios	Lesson 8	Lesson 8	
20.	£6.09	Multiplying money	Lesson 13		
21.	1.6km	Perimeter of irregular shapes	Lesson 11	Lesson 11	
22.	B	Rotational symmetry			Shape builder in *Practise & Pass 11+ Level One: Discover Non-verbal Reasoning* page 76
23.	56	Simple multiples (see Further help p. 29)			
24.	6	Simple division and multiplication (see Further help p. 28)			

25.	£3.85	Handling data/ multiplying money/ subtracting	Lesson 13	Lessons 1 and 12	
26.	85%	Changing fractions to percentages	Lesson 6	Lesson 6	
27.	£12.95	Finding a percentage of a number/ subtraction	Lesson 15	Lessons 1 and 15	
28.	4	Handling data, using averages	Lesson 14	Lessons 12 and 14	
29.	13.5cm	Multiplying, metric measures	Page 124 (metric measures)	Lesson 13	
30.	175g	Using number lines (see Further help p. 31)			
31.	P (2,8) Q (4,3) R (9,7)	Coordinates (see Further help p. 28)			
32.	s + 12t	Algebraic formulae (see Further help p.28)			
33.	57	Finding a percentage of a number	Lesson 15	Lesson 15	
34.	57cm^2	Area of irregular shapes	Lesson 11	Lesson 11	
35.	x = 9	Substitution			*Practise & Pass 11+ Level One: Discover Verbal Reasoning* lesson 13
36.	48	Simple multiplication and subtraction		Lesson 1	
37.	C	Using fractions/ percentages	Lessons 2 and 15	Lessons 2 and 15	
38.	C	Calculating probability	Lesson 7	Lesson 7	
39.	E	Angles	Lesson 12		
40.	£9.34	Adding, subtracting with decimals	Lesson 5		

41.	trapezium	Names of shapes (see Further help p. 29)			
42.	C	Directions, angles	Lesson 12		
43.	16	Handling data		Lesson 12	
44.	3km	Ratio	Lesson 8	Lesson 8	
45.	E	Proportion	Lesson 9	Lesson 9	
46.	10.5cm^2	Areas of irregular shapes	Lesson 11	Lesson 11	
47.	45°	Angles	Lesson 12		
48.	B	Properties of shapes (see Further help p. 29)			
49.	D	Long multiplication, subtraction		Lessons 1 and 13	
50.	C	Decision trees (see Further help p. 30)			

Practice Paper 2: Question types and further practice references

Question	Answer	Type of question	*Practise & Pass 11+ Level One: Discover Maths* lessons to refer to for further practice	*Practise & Pass 11+ Level Two: Develop Maths* lessons to refer to for further practice	Other titles in the *Practise & Pass 11+* series to refer to
1.	100	Place value	Lesson 1		
2.	19	Handling data		Lesson 12	
3.	34,722	Place value	Lesson 1		
4.	12	Number machines, using subtraction and division		Lesson 1	
5.	134	Division, multiplying with money	Lesson 13		
6.	D	Turning fractions into decimals and percentages	Lesson 6	Lesson 6	
7.	18	Handling data, using averages	Lesson 14	Lessons 12 and 14	
8.	12	Finding area of irregular shapes and triangles	Lesson 11	Lesson 11	
9.	£105	Proportion	Lesson 9	Lesson 9	
10.	E	Rotational symmetry			Shape builder in *Practise & Pass 11+ Level One: Discover Non-verbal Reasoning* page 76
11.	58	Using subtraction		Lesson 1	
12.	-12°C	Negative numbers (see Further help p. 30)			
13.	D	Prime numbers			*Practise & Pass 11+ Level One: Discover Verbal Reasoning* lesson 12

15

14.	C	Coordinates (see Further help p. 28)			
15.	32	Logic problems			*Practise & Pass 11+ Level Two: Develop Verbal Reasoning lesson 10*
16.	E	Several ways to solve this, such as compare equivalent fractions or turn them all into percentages.	Lesson 6	Lesson 6	
17.	B	Metric measures	Page 124		
18.	28	Fractions of a whole number	Lesson 2	Lesson 2	
19.	£19.74	Multiplying money and larger numbers	Lesson 13	Lesson 13	
20.	£32	Long division, multiplying money, larger numbers	Lesson 13	Lesson 13	
21.	6	Using averages	Lesson 14	Lesson 14	
22.	A	Algebraic formulae – simple ratios can help with this.	Lesson 8	Lesson 8	
23.	£1,237.50	Multiplying money, larger numbers	Lesson 13	Lesson 13	
24.	47.5m	Perimeter and ratio	Lessons 8 and 10	Lessons 8 and 10	
25.	$\frac{1}{7}$	Probability	Lesson 7	Lesson 7	

26.	A	Coordinates and quadrilaterals (see Further help p. 28)			
27.	14th	Multiplying decimals and metric measures	Lesson 13 and page 124		
28.	hexagon	2D shapes, reflective symmetry			Shape builder in *Practise & Pass 11+ Level One: Discover Non-verbal Reasoning* page 16
29.	E	Properties of shapes (see Further help p. 29)			
30.	Q and S	Angles	Lesson 12		
31.	B	Ratio and simplifying fractions	Lessons 4 and 8	Lessons 4 and 8	
32.	11	Prime numbers			*Practise & Pass 11+ Level One: Discover Verbal Reasoning* lesson 12
33.	300	Ratios	Lesson 8	Lesson 8	
34.	2,118km	Fractions of a whole number	Lesson 2	Lesson 2	
35.	53.25kg	Using averages	Lesson 14	Lesson 14	
36.	120°	Finding angles	Lesson 12		
37.	59,400	Multiplying larger numbers		Lesson 13	
38.	25%	Turning fractions into percentages	Lesson 6	Lesson 6	
39.	$x = 3$	Solving algebraic equations (see Further help p. 27)			

40.	75x + 30y	Algebraic formulae (see Further help p. 28)			
41.	£59.00	Multiplying money, subtracting with decimals	Lessons 5 and 13		
42.	34m²	Area of irregular shapes	Lesson 11	Lesson 11	
43.	90	Handling data, ratios	Lesson 8	Lessons 8 and 12	
44.	£91.80	Finding percentage of a number, subtracting decimals	Lessons 5 and 15	Lesson 15	
45.	10km	Ratio	Lesson 8	Lesson 8	
46.	20cm²	Area of regular and irregular shapes, using averages	Lessons 10, 11 and 14	Lessons 11 and 14	
47.	16	Area of irregular shapes	Lesson 11	Lesson 11	
48.	C	Directions (see Further help p. 30)			
49.	4j + 4h + 60	Algebraic formulae (see Further help p. 28)			
50.	4(XY/2)	Area of irregular shapes	Lesson 11	Lesson 11	

Practice paper 3: question types and further practice references

Question	Answer	Type of question	*Practise & Pass 11+ Level One: Discover Maths* lessons to refer to for further practice	*Practise & Pass 11+ Level Two: Develop Maths* lessons to refer to for further practice	Other titles in the *Practise & Pass 11+* series to refer to
1.	D	Place value	Lesson 1		
2.	46	Using subtraction		Lesson 1	
3.	C	24 hour clock, adding decimals	Lesson 5		
4.	C	Reflective symmetry			Shape builder in *Practise & Pass 11+ Level One: Discover Non-verbal Reasoning* page 16
5.	10.5m	Proportion	Lesson 9	Lesson 9	
6.	10,304	Long multiplication		Lesson 13	
7.	Fajer	Square numbers			*Practise & Pass 11+ Level One: Discover Verbal Reasoning* lesson 12
8.	obtuse	Angles	Lesson 12		
9.	$\frac{1}{9}$	Simplifying fractions	Lesson 4	Lesson 4	
10.	C	Handling data		Lesson 12	
11.	80	Simple multiples (see Further help p. 29)			
12.	2	Using averages, subtraction	Lesson 14	Lessons 1 and 14	
13.	60°	Angles	Lesson 12	Lesson 12	
14.	22.4	Adding decimals and using number lines	Lesson 5		

15.	E	Coordinates (see Further help p. 28)			
16.	27	Ratios	Lesson 8	Lesson 8	
17.	21p	Multiplying money, adding, subtracting decimals	Lessons 5 and 13		
18.	3	Angles	Lesson 12		
19.	B	Coordinates (see Further help p. 28)			
20.	D	Simple multiplication, subtraction (see Further help p. 28)			
21.	E	Ratios	Lesson 8	Lesson 8	
22.	57°	Angles, subtraction	Lesson 12	Lesson 1	
23.	(7,5)	Coordinates (see Further help p. 28)			
24.	30	Averages	Lesson 14	Lesson 14	
25.	£108	Proportion, adding and multiplying decimals	Lessons 5 and 9	Lesson 9	
26.	24	Simple division (see Further help p. 28)			
27.	$\frac{5}{8}$	Using probability	Lesson 7	Lesson 7	
28.	12	Logic problems			*Practise & Pass 11+ Level Two: Develop Verbal Reasoning* lesson 10
29.	0.77	Handling data, subtracting decimals	Lesson 5	Lesson 12	
30.	B	Turning fractions into decimals, percentages	Lesson 6	Lesson 6	

31.	57	Ratios	Lesson 8	Lesson 8	
32.	2	Reflective and rotational symmetry			Shape builders in *Practise & Pass 11+ Level One: Discover Non-verbal Reasoning* pages 16 and 76
33.	£22	Percentages of numbers, division	Lesson 15	Lesson 15	
34.	200cm²	Using area	Lesson 10		
35.	C	Using area and perimeter	Lesson 10		
36.	24	Proportion	Lesson 9	Lesson 9	
37.	16.5km	Proportion, using metric measures	Lesson 9 and p124 (metric measures)	Lesson 9	
38.	E	Turning fractions into decimals, percentages will help compare	Lesson 6	Lesson 6	
39.	C	Algebraic equations, use simple ratios to help compare	Lesson 8	Lesson 8	
40.	14.4 litres	Long multiplication and subtraction		Lessons 1 and 13	
41.	127	Simple addition, subtraction		Lesson 1	
42.	1.14 pounds	Handling data, adding decimals	Lesson 5	Lesson 12	
43.	£23.94	Multiplying money	Lesson 13		
44.	A	Use ratio and proportion to help solve	Lessons 8 and 9	Lessons 8 and 9	

45.	£24.50	Multiplying money, adding decimals	Lessons 5 and 13		
46.	C	Converting metric to imperial. 1 inch = 2.5cm so also multiplying decimals	Lesson 13		
47.	D	Turning fractions to decimals, percentages for comparison	Lesson 6	Lesson 6	
48.	15x + 10y	Algebraic formulae (see Further help p. 28)			
49.	E	Angles, shapes	Lesson 12		
50.	D	Directions (see Further help p. 30)			

Practice paper 4: question types and further practice references

Question	Answer	Type of question	*Practise & Pass 11+ Level One: Discover Maths* lessons to refer to for further practice	*Practise & Pass 11+ Level Two: Develop Maths* lessons to refer to for further practice	Other titles in the *Practise & Pass 11+* series to refer to
1.	2,995	Subtraction		Lesson 1	
2.	21 to 24	Handling data		Lesson 12	
3.	C	Estimating capacity (see Further help p. 30)			
4.	126	Simple multiplication, addition (see Further help p. 28)			
5.	Tuesday	Simple multiples (see Further help p. 29)			
6.	£35.54	Subtracting decimals, subtraction	Lesson 5	Lesson 1	
7.	2,730	Subtraction		Lesson 1	
8.	0.8m	Subtracting decimals	Lesson 5		
9.	26,988	Multiplying larger numbers		Lesson 13	
10.	B	Simple multiples (see Further help p. 29)			
11.	D	Rotational symmetry			Shape builder in *Practise & Pass 11+ Level One: Discover Non-verbal Reasoning* page 76
12.	2p	Multiplying, subtracting decimals	Lesson 13		

13.	£6.27	Multiplying money, adding decimals	Lesson 13		
14.	52	Finding percentages of numbers	Lesson 15	Lesson 15	
15.	(1.5, 1.2)	Coordinates (see Further help p. 28)			
16.	8	Simple multiplication (see Further help p. 28)			
17.	£126	Proportion	Lesson 9	Lesson 9	
18.	28m	Proportion	Lesson 9	Lesson 9	
19.	D	Road/path networks (see Further help p. 31)			
20.	(4,9)	Coordinates (see Further help p. 28)			
21.	D	Properties of shapes (see Further help p. 29)			
22.	1 and 2	Handling data		Lesson 12	
23.	5	Simple division (see Further help p. 28)			
24.	6.5	Adding decimals	Lesson 5		
25.	100	Fractions of a whole number	Lesson 2	Lesson 2	
26.	17	Number patterns			*Practise & Pass 11+ Level One: Discover Verbal Reasoning* Lesson 12
27.	Q and R	Reflective, rotational symmetry			Shape builders in *Practise & Pass 11+ Level One: Discover Non-verbal Reasoning* pages 16 and 76

28.	20%	Probability, turning fractions into percentages	Lessons 6 and 7	Lessons 6 and 7	
29.	162	Multiplying larger numbers	Lesson 13		
30.	30	Working out combinations (see Further help p. 32)			
31.	D	Coordinates and names of shapes (see Further help p. 28 and p. 29)			
32.	37.5%	Turning fractions into percentages	Lesson 6	Lesson 6	
33.	$x + 5 + 4$	Algebraic formulae (see Further help p. 28)			
34.	E	Place value	Lesson 1		
35.	D	Decision trees (see Further help p. 30)			
36.	£5.60	Proportion, subtracting decimals	Lessons 5 and 9	Lesson 9	
37.	D	Converting metric and imperial measures, also multiplying decimals as 1 inch = 2.5cm	Lesson 13		
38.	C	Probability	Lesson 7	Lesson 7	
39.	8.25	Rounding decimals		Lesson 5	
40.	$x = 3$	Algebraic formulae (see Further help p. 28)			

41.	£149.75	Area of irregular shapes, multiplying decimals, larger numbers	Lessons 11 and 13	Lessons 11 and 13	
42.	18cm^2	Area of irregular shapes	Lesson 11	Lesson 11	
43.	B	Multiples, factors, prime numbers	Lesson 4 (factors)		
44.	C	Directions (see Further help p. 30)			
45.	D	Simple multiples (see Further help p. 29)			
46.	20cm^2	Area of irregular shapes	Lesson 11	Lesson 11	
47.	27	Calculating volume		Lesson 10	
48.	8	Averages and ranges	Lesson 14	Lesson 14	
49.	$c^2 + 4(cd)$	Algebraic expressions, area of irregular shapes	Lesson 11	Lesson 11	
50.	20	Proportion	Lesson 9	Lesson 9	

FURTHER HELP

The following pages contain further help and advice on question types not included in Level One and Level Two titles.

ALGEBRA

Anyone looking at the tests will notice algebra questions. Some of these can be very tricky and many students will not have learnt these in school.

Instead of covering several types of algebra the best method is to use the multiple choice answers – trying to introduce the concept of algebra may well confuse students further. Look at the example below to see how to use the multiple choice options.

Question: If $3x + 17 = 26$, what is x?

A	1
B	2
C	3
D	4
E	5

3x means 3 multiplied by whatever x is so instruct the student to try each multiple choice option in turn.

Try answer A first, $x = 1$.
3 times 1 would mean $3 + 17 = 20$.

This cannot be correct since the answer must equal 26 so try the next option.

Answer B, $x = 2$
3 times 2 is 6. $6 + 17 = 23$.

This cannot be correct either so try the next option.

Answer C, $x = 3$
3 times $3 = 9$. $9 + 17 = 26$.

That's correct so the answer must be C.

Trying each answer in this way should help students. There are many different types of algebra question but advising the student to try all of the answers to see which gives the most sensible answer is the easiest and fastest way of tackling these questions.

ALGEBRAIC FORMULAE

For questions which require students to create an algebraic formula, simply read the question carefully and work out which numbers can be calculated.

For example:

Question: If Brian eats y pies every day for 3 weeks, how many does he eat?

In this case we can work out that Brian eats 7 days a week for 3 weeks which is $3 \times 7 = 21$ days.

Since we only know the pies as y each day our answer must be that Brian eats 21y pies.

SIMPLE DIVISION AND MULTIPLICATION

For simple multiplication type questions, students should make good use of their knowledge of multiplication facts.

For example: $9 \times 8 = 72$ (students should know this without having to calculate it).

For simple division questions students should already be aware that division is the inverse operation of multiplication. So students should make good use of their knowledge of multiplication facts to help calculate division questions quickly and accurately.

For example, if a question requires a student to divide 96 by 12, it should be remembered that $12 \times 8 = 96$ so using this knowledge it follows that $96 \div 12 = 8$.

COORDINATES

For coordinate questions, students need to remember that the horizontal (x axis) coordinate is always plotted before the vertical (y axis) coordinate. Students should be particularly wary when faced with multiple choice options which will present similar looking answer options.

For example: the coordinate (6, 2) means go along the horizontal x axis 6 then up the vertical y axis 2.

Students could easily confuse this with the coordinate (2, 6) so remind them to take care!

NUMBER MACHINES

Number machines are a way of showing number sentences in a different way. It's important that students check whether they are asked to find the number to put in or the number which comes out.

For example, a number machine may say that the number put in is multiplied by 2 then has 3 added to it. If the number put in is 9 then this would be $9 \times 2 = 18 + 3 = 21$.

However, if students are told the number which comes out is 21 then they will need to do the inverse calculation so $21 - 3 = 18 \div 2 = 9$.

Students may also be told that the number put in is 14 and the answer is 42, so what happened to it in the number machine? In this case advise students to look at the multiple choice options and find the one which will give the correct answer. In this case the answer is 'multiply by 3' since $14 \times 3 = 42$.

SIMPLE MULTIPLES

All students should know how to find multiples of numbers. Simply put, it means find all the multiplication answers for a number.

For example: the first 5 multiples of 7 would be 7, 14, 21, 28 and 35.

NAMES OF SHAPES

Students need to ensure that they know the names of all 2 dimensional or plane shapes up to and including decagons (10-sided shapes) and how many sides each has.

They also need to know the names of different types of quadrilaterals and triangles (see lesson 12 in *Practise & Pass 11+: Discover Maths* for information on triangles).

Students should also know the names of common 3 dimensional or solid shapes (such as cube, trapezoid).

PROPERTIES OF SHAPES

As well as knowing the names of the shapes discussed above, students also need to know the properties of all of them. It's really important that students know that edges, faces and vertices are all different and how to identify each in 3 dimensional shapes.

They should already know about sides and corners of 2 dimensional shapes.

For example, a square has 4 sides and 4 corners while a cube has 6 faces, 12 edges and 8 vertices.

NEGATIVE NUMBERS

Students at this level need to understand that numbers can be negative. Questions which typically employ negative numbers are those involving temperatures or coordinates.

For example: if the temperature in a city is 3° and it drops by 7°, the new temperature is
3 − 7 = −4°

DIRECTIONS

Students are expected to know directions in the form of compass points, including the main 8 points. A good way to remember the main 4 is the mnemonic Naughty Elephants Spray Water – which stands for North, East, South and West working in a clockwise direction.

Additionally students need to know how to give directions using instructions such as 'turn left 90°', 'move forward 3' as though using squares on a grid.

Encourage students to try turning the paper round to help them see which direction to travel next.

DECISION TREES

When answering questions using decision trees, students simply need to take care to read each section of the tree correctly. It's important for them to look at the 'empty' box and work out whether the answer to its question is a 'yes' or a 'no' and look at the final result. This will make working out the missing question quite straightforward.

For example: if the answer to the empty box is 'yes' and the final result is 'blue paper' then the missing question would need to be 'Is the paper blue?' If however, the answer was 'no' then the question would need to be 'Is the paper red?'

ESTIMATING CAPACITY/HEIGHT/LENGTH OR DISTANCE/WEIGHT

These questions can be really tricky in that they are sometimes difficult to work out. The best thing to do is to advise students to rule out answers from the multiple choice options that are clearly too small or too large. Also, if any of the answers are the same amount but written in a different way, they are also incorrect (for example, if 1 litre and 1000ml are listed as answers, these are the same so could not be correct as only one answer will be correct).

To improve estimating ability, try advising students to help parents unpack shopping, taking care to look at the different weights/capacity of common household items such as drinks bottles, tins etc. In this way students can build up a knowledge of what items hold and weigh.

ROAD/PATH NETWORKS

For questions involving roads/paths which can only be used once but must all be used, there are two useful rules.

1. A set of paths whereby there is an even number of paths at all the junctions (where the paths meet) will always work.
2. A set of paths containing only two junctions with an odd number of paths will work.

So students need only to count the paths meeting at each junction and find the one with even numbers and that will be the answer.

CONVERTING METRIC TO IMPERIAL

Students need to know some of the more common conversions so that they can at least make an estimated conversion.

Ensure that students know the following conversions to 1 decimal place.

- 2.5cm = 1 inch
- 1.6km = 1 mile
- 1 kilogram = 2.2 pounds
- 0.6 (0.57) litres = 1 pint

USING NUMBER LINES

When using number lines, it is important for students to identify the amounts that the number line is increasing by. The best way to do this is to count the jumps between numbers then split the amount by this number.

For example:

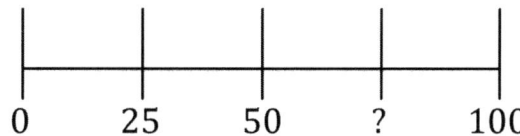

On the number line above there are 4 jumps between 0 and 100 so 100 ÷ 4 = 25. This tells us each line is worth an extra 25 so the missing number should be 50 + 25 = 75.

WORKING OUT COMBINATIONS

To work out all the different possible combinations for questions that give several variables, we can simply multiply the number of each.

For example: if a question explains that there are 2 types of hat, 3 types of coat and 4 types of shoes then asks how many different combinations are possible, we simply multiply all 3 numbers.

So 2 × 3 × 4 = 24.

There are many different types of problems like this. Students should try to set out information in an organised way so they can identify patterns more easily.

PRACTISE & PASS 11+

MATHS
ANSWER GRIDS

Students should mark their answers to the practice papers in this answer booklet.

Contents

Practice paper 1	3
Practice paper 2	5
Practice paper 3	7
Practice paper 4	9

© Peter Williams and Trotman Publishing, 2015

The right of Peter Williams to be identified as the author of this work has been asserted by him in accordance with the Copyright, Designs and Patents Act, 1988.

All rights reserved. No part of this publication may be transmitted in any form or by any means, or stored in a retrieval system without prior written permission from the publisher.

First published 2015 by Trotman Publishing, a division of Crimson Publishing Ltd, 19–21c Charles Street, Bath BA1 1HX.

ISBN 978 1 84455 428 7

A catalogue record for this book is available from the British Library.

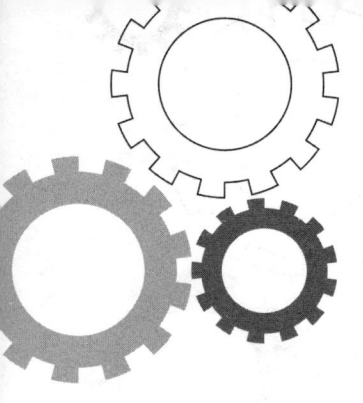

PRACTICE PAPER 1

Student's name

School name

Date of test

Please mark answers like this ⊟

1
- 3
- 30
- 300
- 3000
- 3/100

2
- 6
- 7
- 9
- 5 to 10
- 6 to 9

3
- 560
- 160
- 360
- 3240
- 80

4
- 73%
- 27%
- 33%
- 77%
- 37%

5
- £487.50
- £19.25
- £7.80
- £78.00
- £0.78

6
- 24cm
- 3.75cm
- 37.5cm
- 2.2cm
- 3/8cm

7
- 156
- 276
- 120
- 211.5
- 209

8
- 102
- 395
- 1,580
- 1,717
- 1,817

9
- A
- B
- C
- D
- E

10
- (30, 10)
- (10, 30)
- (20, 15)
- (15, 20)
- (30, 20)

11
- 6
- 12
- 15
- 75
- 20

12
- 6cm²
- 42cm²
- 54cm²
- 27cm²
- 15cm²

13
- 70
- 35
- 108
- 82
- 234

14
- 2
- 3
- 4
- 5
- 6

15
- 23.3cm
- 23.4cm
- 23.34cm
- 23.35cm
- 23.5cm

16
- A
- B
- C
- D
- E

17
- x − 8 years
- x − 3 to 5 years
- x + 3 years
- x + 5 years
- x + 8 years

18
- 56
- 14
- 91
- 18
- 44

19
- £73
- £52
- £59
- £66
- £104

20
- £1.20
- £60.90
- £6.09
- £11.31
- £17.40

21
- 1.6km
- 15.1km
- 1.51km
- 16km
- 29.5km

22
- A
- B
- C
- D
- E

23
- 11
- 35
- 21
- 44
- 56

24
- 210
- 21
- 6
- 28
- 14

25
- £3.10
- £3.85
- £3.15
- £3.45
- £38.50

26	27	28	29	30
17% ☐	£5.55 ☐	2 ☐	12cm ☐	150g ☐
20% ☐	£1.85 ☐	3 ☐	135cm ☐	160g ☐
3% ☐	£12.95 ☐	4 ☐	12.8cm ☐	180g ☐
85% ☐	£13.05 ☐	5 ☐	13.5cm ☐	175g ☐
15% ☐	£16.65 ☐	6 ☐	13cm ☐	155g ☐

31	32	33	34	35
P (2,8) Q (3,4) R (9,7) ☐	12st ☐	38 ☐	42cm² ☐	$x = 9$ ☐
P (2,8) Q (4,3) R (9,7) ☐	12 + s + t ☐	19 ☐	30cm² ☐	$x = 12$ ☐
P (8,2) Q (3,4) R (7,9) ☐	12s + t ☐	323 ☐	15cm² ☐	$x = 21$ ☐
P (2,8) Q (9,7) R (4,3) ☐	s + 12t ☐	295 ☐	57cm² ☐	$x = 5$ ☐
P (8,2) Q (4,3) R (7,9) ☐	12(s + t) ☐	57 ☐	72cm² ☐	$x = 24$ ☐

36	37	38	39	40
4 ☐	A ☐	A ☐	A ☐	£7.67 ☐
16 ☐	B ☐	B ☐	B ☐	£9.34 ☐
64 ☐	C ☐	C ☐	C ☐	£3.34 ☐
80 ☐	D ☐	D ☐	D ☐	£11.50 ☐
48 ☐	E ☐	E ☐	E ☐	£21.67 ☐

41	42	43	44	45
rectangle ☐	A ☐	25 ☐	3km ☐	A ☐
kite ☐	B ☐	16 ☐	1.5km ☐	B ☐
parallelogram ☐	C ☐	7 ☐	3000km ☐	C ☐
square ☐	D ☐	5 ☐	2000m ☐	D ☐
trapezium ☐	E ☐	4 ☐	3m ☐	E ☐

46	47	48	49	50
9cm² ☐	90° ☐	A ☐	A ☐	A ☐
9.5cm² ☐	180° ☐	B ☐	B ☐	B ☐
10cm² ☐	45° ☐	C ☐	C ☐	C ☐
10.5cm² ☐	60° ☐	D ☐	D ☐	D ☐
11cm² ☐	30° ☐	E ☐	E ☐	E ☐

PRACTICE PAPER 2

Student's name

School name

Date of test

Please mark answers like this ⊟

1	2	3	4	5
7 ☐	19 ☐	37,422 ☐	119 ☐	136 ☐
70 ☐	48 ☐	34,272 ☐	12 ☐	134 ☐
700 ☐	29 ☐	34,227 ☐	18 ☐	13 ☐
100 ☐	26 ☐	34,702 ☐	84 ☐	16 ☐
63 ☐	22 ☐	34,722 ☐	77 ☐	34 ☐

6	7	8	9	10
A ☐	90 ☐	6 ☐	£42 ☐	A ☐
B ☐	18 ☐	10 ☐	£15 ☐	B ☐
C ☐	85 ☐	12 ☐	£52 ☐	C ☐
D ☐	24 ☐	36 ☐	£105 ☐	D ☐
E ☐	30 ☐	30 ☐	£315 ☐	E ☐

11	12	13	14	15
542 ☐	12°C ☐	A ☐	A ☐	32 ☐
463 ☐	26°C ☐	B ☐	B ☐	33 ☐
195 ☐	−12°C ☐	C ☐	C ☐	28 ☐
1142 ☐	−11°C ☐	D ☐	D ☐	24 ☐
58 ☐	−7°C ☐	E ☐	E ☐	36 ☐

16	17	18	19	20
A ☐	A ☐	20 ☐	£0.94 ☐	£3.32 ☐
B ☐	B ☐	72 ☐	£1.41 ☐	£32 ☐
C ☐	C ☐	21 ☐	£6.58 ☐	£86,528 ☐
D ☐	D ☐	28 ☐	£3.29 ☐	£138 ☐
E ☐	E ☐	40 ☐	£19.74 ☐	£30 ☐

21	22	23	24	25
6 ☐	A ☐	£1,237.50 ☐	2.75m ☐	4/10 ☐
4.5 ☐	B ☐	£137.50 ☐	19cm ☐	2/5 ☐
7 ☐	C ☐	£247.50 ☐	4750m ☐	2/12 ☐
5.5 ☐	D ☐	£45.00 ☐	2750m ☐	1/6 ☐
25.5 ☐	E ☐	£385.00 ☐	47.5m ☐	1/7 ☐

26	27	28	29	30
A ☐	10th ☐	rectangle ☐	A ☐	P and R ☐
B ☐	11th ☐	pentagon ☐	B ☐	P and S ☐
C ☐	12th ☐	hexagon ☐	C ☐	Q and T ☐
D ☐	13th ☐	trapezium ☐	D ☐	Q and S ☐
E ☐	14th ☐	octagon ☐	E ☐	R and T ☐

31	32	33	34	35
A ☐	11 ☐	72 ☐	1,647km ☐	53.25kg ☐
B ☐	9 ☐	60 ☐	706km ☐	48.52kg ☐
C ☐	7 ☐	300 ☐	235km ☐	45.85kg ☐
D ☐	5 ☐	1800 ☐	2,118km ☐	55.32kg ☐
E ☐	3 ☐	66 ☐	988km ☐	48.2kg ☐

36	37	38	39	40
60° ☐	45,000 ☐	30% ☐	$x = 2$ ☐	$15x + 15y$ ☐
180° ☐	59,400 ☐	10% ☐	$x = 3$ ☐	$15(10x + y)$ ☐
360° ☐	2,294 ☐	20% ☐	$x = 4$ ☐	$15(5x + 2y)$ ☐
120° ☐	7,190 ☐	25% ☐	$x = 5$ ☐	$75x + 30y$ ☐
300° ☐	6,750 ☐	33% ☐	$x = 6$ ☐	$15x + 30y$ ☐

41	42	43	44	45
£44.50 ☐	34m^2 ☐	20 ☐	£10.80 ☐	1km ☐
£64.50 ☐	36m^2 ☐	80 ☐	£102.60 ☐	10km ☐
£59.00 ☐	30m^2 ☐	45 ☐	£97.20 ☐	100km ☐
£66.00 ☐	40m^2 ☐	90 ☐	£16.20 ☐	1000km ☐
£16.00 ☐	32m^2 ☐	135 ☐	£91.80 ☐	10000km ☐

46	47	48	49	50
18cm^2 ☐	10 ☐	A ☐	$4j + 4h + 60$ ☐	XY ☐
19cm^2 ☐	12 ☐	B ☐	$4(hj) + 60$ ☐	4XY ☐
20cm^2 ☐	14 ☐	C ☐	$4(hj60)$ ☐	6XY ☐
21cm^2 ☐	16 ☐	D ☐	$h + 4j + 60$ ☐	$4(XY/2)$ ☐
22cm^2 ☐	18 ☐	E ☐	$4(h \times j) + 60$ ☐	$4X + 4Y$ ☐

PRACTICE PAPER 3

Student's name

School name

Date of test

Please mark answers like this ⊟

1
- A
- B
- C
- D
- E

2
- 112
- 270
- 46
- 49
- 36

3
- A
- B
- C
- D
- E

4
- A
- B
- C
- D
- E

5
- 10.5m
- 10m
- 9m
- 12m
- 14m

6
- 3,680
- 2,944
- 396
- 7,360
- 10,304

7
- Phillip
- Mercedes
- Fajer
- Emma
- Mike

8
- acute
- obtuse
- right
- reflex
- straight

9
- 1/4
- 1/5
- 1/7
- 1/9
- 1/10

10
- A
- B
- C
- D
- E

11
- 5
- 10
- 20
- 40
- 80

12
- 2
- 23
- 25
- 3
- 5

13
- 120°
- 90°
- 180°
- 360°
- 60°

14
- 24
- 23
- 22.2
- 22.4
- 22.5

15
- A
- B
- C
- D
- E

16
- 18
- 12
- 54
- 27
- 9

17
- 36p
- 77p
- 66p
- 21p
- £1.79

18
- 1
- 2
- 3
- 4
- 5

19
- A
- B
- C
- D
- E

20
- A
- B
- C
- D
- E

21
- A
- B
- C
- D
- E

22
- 237°
- 57°
- 180°
- 45°
- 60°

23
- (4,3)
- (5,7)
- (3,4)
- (6,6)
- (7,5)

24
- 30
- 102
- 132
- 28
- 22

25
- £43.20
- £98
- £9
- £108
- £10.80

26		27		28		29		30	
890	☐	2/4	☐	14	☐	10.03	☐	A	☐
23	☐	1/2	☐	7	☐	0.77	☐	B	☐
22	☐	1/4	☐	9 1/2	☐	10.8	☐	C	☐
24	☐	3/8	☐	12	☐	10.35	☐	D	☐
97	☐	5/8	☐	5	☐	0.83	☐	E	☐

31		32		33		34		35	
19	☐	0	☐	£30	☐	200cm^2	☐	A	☐
57	☐	1	☐	£330	☐	2m^2	☐	B	☐
38	☐	2	☐	£2	☐	33cm^2	☐	C	☐
25	☐	3	☐	£20	☐	2000cm^2	☐	D	☐
72	☐	4	☐	£22	☐	0.2m^2	☐	E	☐

36		37		38		39		40	
15	☐	3km	☐	A	☐	A	☐	1.5 litres	☐
16	☐	5.5km	☐	B	☐	B	☐	15 litres	☐
8	☐	1.65km	☐	C	☐	C	☐	14.4 litres	☐
24	☐	15.5km	☐	D	☐	D	☐	6 litres	☐
32	☐	16.5km	☐	E	☐	E	☐	3.6 litres	☐

41		42		43		44		45	
1	☐	3.76 pounds	☐	£23.94	☐	A	☐	£5.13	☐
63	☐	1.14 pounds	☐	£9.99	☐	B	☐	£82.35	☐
86	☐	0.38 pounds	☐	£4.05	☐	C	☐	£24.50	☐
127	☐	1.90 pounds	☐	£47.88	☐	D	☐	£21.25	☐
41	☐	1.04 pounds	☐	£23.99	☐	E	☐	£13.20	☐

46		47		48		49		50	
A	☐	A	☐	15x + 10y	☐	A	☐	A	☐
B	☐	B	☐	3x + 2y	☐	B	☐	B	☐
C	☐	C	☐	5x + 5y	☐	C	☐	C	☐
D	☐	D	☐	5(3y + 2x)	☐	D	☐	D	☐
E	☐	E	☐	10x + 10y	☐	E	☐	E	☐

PRACTICE PAPER 4

Student's name

School name

Date of test

Please mark answers like this ▭

1	2	3	4	5
3,005 ▢	25 ▢	A ▢	126 ▢	Monday ▢
2,995 ▢	21 to 24 ▢	B ▢	42 ▢	Tuesday ▢
63,141 ▢	15 to 20 ▢	C ▢	63 ▢	Wednesday ▢
2,095 ▢	25 to 30 ▢	D ▢	54 ▢	Thursday ▢
3,051 ▢	21 ▢	E ▢	45 ▢	Friday ▢

6	7	8	9	10
£36.25 ▢	13,270 ▢	0.8m ▢	424 ▢	A ▢
£38.54 ▢	273 ▢	7.6m ▢	5,190 ▢	B ▢
£36.91 ▢	2,740 ▢	−0.8m ▢	24,220 ▢	C ▢
£35.54 ▢	12,295 ▢	1.2m ▢	26,988 ▢	D ▢
£36.54 ▢	2,730 ▢	8cm ▢	27,680 ▢	E ▢

11	12	13	14	15
A ▢	26p ▢	£1.65 ▢	65 ▢	(1.2, 1.5) ▢
B ▢	2p ▢	£4.22 ▢	45 ▢	(1.4, 1.4) ▢
C ▢	£3.38 ▢	£5.87 ▢	13 ▢	(1.5, 1.5) ▢
D ▢	27p ▢	£1.87 ▢	6.5 ▢	(1.5, 1.2) ▢
E ▢	1p ▢	£6.27 ▢	52 ▢	(1.2, 1.6) ▢

16	17	18	19	20
6 ▢	£42 ▢	16m ▢	A ▢	(4,8) ▢
7 ▢	£56 ▢	14m ▢	B ▢	(9,4) ▢
8 ▢	£24 ▢	28m ▢	C ▢	(8,4) ▢
9 ▢	£126 ▢	22m ▢	D ▢	(3,9) ▢
10 ▢	£84 ▢	21m ▢	E ▢	(4,9) ▢

21	22	23	24	25
A ▢	10 and 11 ▢	225 ▢	6.1 ▢	20 ▢
B ▢	11 and 12 ▢	25 ▢	7 ▢	12 ▢
C ▢	12 and 1 ▢	5 ▢	6.5 ▢	100 ▢
D ▢	1 and 2 ▢	15 ▢	6.75 ▢	30 ▢
E ▢	2 and 3 ▢	1,875 ▢	6.2 ▢	60 ▢

26		27		28		29		30	
	15 ☐		P and R ☐		10% ☐		162 ☐		10 ☐
	17 ☐		Q and S ☐		15% ☐		72 ☐		6 ☐
	19 ☐		P and T ☐		20% ☐		54 ☐		15 ☐
	21 ☐		Q and S ☐		25% ☐		18 ☐		30 ☐
	23 ☐		Q and R ☐		30% ☐		6 ☐		25 ☐

31		32		33		34		35	
	A ☐		25% ☐		$x \times 9$ ☐		A ☐		A ☐
	B ☐		30% ☐		$x - 9$ ☐		B ☐		B ☐
	C ☐		35% ☐		$x + 4 - 5$ ☐		C ☐		C ☐
	D ☐		37.5% ☐		$x + 5 + 4$ ☐		D ☐		D ☐
	E ☐		40% ☐		$x - 5 - 4$ ☐		E ☐		E ☐

36		37		38		39		40	
	£18.40 ☐		A ☐		A ☐		8.2 ☐		$x = 2$ ☐
	£6.40 ☐		B ☐		B ☐		8.3 ☐		$x = 3$ ☐
	£5.60 ☐		C ☐		C ☐		8.26 ☐		$x = 4$ ☐
	£5.40 ☐		D ☐		D ☐		8.25 ☐		$x = 5$ ☐
	£6.60 ☐		E ☐		E ☐		8.24 ☐		$x = 6$ ☐

41		42		43		44		45	
	£30.99 ☐		24cm^2 ☐		A ☐		A ☐		A ☐
	£25.00 ☐		26cm^2 ☐		B ☐		B ☐		B ☐
	£149.99 ☐		12cm^2 ☐		C ☐		C ☐		C ☐
	£149.75 ☐		8cm^2 ☐		D ☐		D ☐		D ☐
	£239.60 ☐		18cm^2 ☐		E ☐		E ☐		E ☐

46		47		48		49		50	
	10cm^2 ☐		5 ☐		7 ☐		$4c + 4d$ ☐		15 ☐
	14cm^2 ☐		15 ☐		8 ☐		$4(c + d)$ ☐		20 ☐
	18cm^2 ☐		9 ☐		9 ☐		$4cd$ ☐		25 ☐
	20cm^2 ☐		18 ☐		10 ☐		$c^2 + 4(cd)$ ☐		5 ☐
	24cm^2 ☐		27 ☐		12 ☐		$4c^2 + 4d^2$ ☐		7 ☐